Microsoft® Office
Excel® 2007

VISUAL™
Quick Tips

Visual®

by Denise Etheridge

1807
WILEY
2007

Wiley Publishing, Inc.

Microsoft® Office Excel® 2007 VISUAL™ Quick Tips

Published by
Wiley Publishing, Inc.
111 River Street
Hoboken, NJ 07030-5774

Published simultaneously in Canada

Copyright © 2007 by Wiley Publishing, Inc.,
Indianapolis, Indiana

Library of Congress Control Number: 2006936752

ISBN: 978-0-470-08971-2

Manufactured in the United States of America

10 9 8 7 6 5 4 3 2

1K/RV/RS/QW/IN

Trademark Acknowledgments

Contact Us

For general information on our other products and services contact our Customer Care Department within the U.S. at 800-762-2974, outside the U.S. at 317-572-3993, or fax 317-572-4002.

For technical support please visit www.wiley.com/techsupport.

WILEY

Wiley Publishing, Inc.

Sales

Contact Wiley
at (800) 762-2974 or
fax (317) 572-4002.

Praise for Visual Books

"I have to praise you and your company on the fine products you turn out. I have twelve Visual books in my house. They were instrumental in helping me pass a difficult computer course. Thank you for creating books that are easy to follow. Keep turning out those quality books."

Gordon Justin (Brielle, NJ)

"What fantastic teaching books you have produced! Congratulations to you and your staff. You deserve the Nobel prize in Education. Thanks for helping me understand computers."

Bruno Tonon (Melbourne, Australia)

"A Picture Is Worth A Thousand Words! If your learning method is by observing or hands-on training, this is the book for you!"

Lorri Pegan-Durastante (Wickliffe, OH)

"Over time, I have bought a number of your 'Read Less - Learn More' books. For me, they are THE way to learn anything easily. I learn easiest using your method of teaching."

José A. Mazón (Cuba, NY)

"You've got a fan for life!! Thanks so much!!"

Kevin P. Quinn (Oakland, CA)

"I have several books from the Visual series and have always found them to be valuable resources."

Stephen P. Miller (Ballston Spa, NY)

"I have several of your Visual books and they are the best I have ever used."

Stanley Clark (Crawfordville, FL)

"Like a lot of other people, I understand things best when I see them visually. Your books really make learning easy and life more fun."

John T. Frey (Cadillac, MI)

"I have quite a few of your Visual books and have been very pleased with all of them. I love the way the lessons are presented!"

Mary Jane Newman (Yorba Linda, CA)

"Thank you, thank you, thank you...for making it so easy for me to break into this high-tech world."

Gay O'Donnell (Calgary, Alberta, Canada)

"I write to extend my thanks and appreciation for your books. They are clear, easy to follow, and straight to the point. Keep up the good work! I bought several of your books and they are just right! No regrets! I will always buy your books because they are the best."

Seward Kollie (Dakar, Senegal)

"I would like to take this time to thank you and your company for producing great and easy-to-learn products. I bought two of your books from a local bookstore, and it was the best investment I've ever made! Thank you for thinking of us ordinary people."

Jeff Eastman (West Des Moines, IA)

"Compliments to the chef!! Your books are extraordinary! Or, simply put, extra-ordinary, meaning way above the rest! THANK YOU THANK YOU THANK YOU! I buy them for friends, family, and colleagues."

Christine J. Manfrin (Castle Rock, CO)

Credits

Project Editor
Tim Borek

Acquisitions Editor
Jody Lefevere

Product Development Supervisor
Courtney Allen

Copy Editor
Marylouise Wiack

Technical Editors
Suzanne Borys
Lee Musick

Editorial Manager
Robyn Siesky

Business Manager
Amy Knies

Editorial Assistant
Laura Sinise

Manufacturing
Allan Conley
Linda Cook
Paul Gilchrist
Jennifer Guynn

Book Design
Kathie Rickard

Production Coordinator
Adrienne Martinez

Layout
Beth Brooks
Jennifer Mayberry
Heather Ryan

Screen Artist
Jill A. Proll

Illustrators
Ronda David-Burroughs
Cheryl Grubbs

Cover Design
Anthony Bunyan

Proofreader
Henry Lazarek

Quality Control
Melanie Hoffman

Indexer
Richard T. Evans

Special Help
Paul McFedries

Vice President and Executive Group Publisher
Richard Swadley

Vice President and Publisher
Barry Pruett

Composition Director
Debbie Stailey

About the Author

Denise Etheridge is a certified public accountant as well as the president and founder of Baycon Group, Inc. She publishes Web sites, provides consulting services on accounting-related software, and authors computer-related books. You can visit `www.baycongroup.com` to view her online tutorials.

To Frederick Douglass Etheridge Senior

Table of Contents

Boosting Efficiency

Name Cells and Ranges 4

Validate with a Validation List 6

Validate with Data Entry Rules 8

Extend a Series with AutoFill 10

Insert Symbols and Special Characters 12

Hide Rows by Grouping and Outlining 14

Add Comments to a Worksheet 16

Let Excel Read Back Data 18

Working with Formulas and Functions

Calculate with the Function Wizard 22

Define a Constant 24

Create Formulas That Include Names 26

Figure Out Loan Terms 28

Determine the Internal Rate of Return 30

Determine the nth Largest Value 32

Create a Conditional Formula 34

Calculate a Conditional Sum 36

Add a Calculator 38

Find Products and Square Roots 40

Perform Time Calculations 42

Perform Date Calculations 44

chapter 3 — Copying, Formatting, and More

Check Formulas for Errors 48

Change Text to Numbers and Then Calculate 50

Convert a Row to a Column 52

Copy with the Office Clipboard 54

Specify How to Paste with Paste Special 56

Create Your Own Style 60

Copy Styles to Another Workbook 62

Conditionally Format a Worksheet 64

Track Changes While Editing 68

Consolidate Worksheets 70

chapter 4 — Manipulating Records

Enter Data with a Form 74

Filter Duplicate Records 76

Perform Simple Sorts and Filters 78

Perform Complex Sorts 80

Perform Complex Filters 82

Filter by Multiple Criteria in the Same Column 84

Subtotal Sorted Data 86

Chart Filtered Data Easily 88

Count Filtered Records 90

Look Up Information in a Worksheet 92

Define Data as a Table 94

Modify a Table Style 96

Exploring Patterns in Data

Create a PivotTable 100

Modify PivotTable Data and Layout 104

Compute Sub- and Grand Totals 106

Create a Calculated Field 108

Hide Columns or Rows in a PivotTable 110

Sort a PivotTable 111

Create a PivotChart 112

Describe Data with Statistics 114

Find the Correlation Between Variables 116

Explore Outcomes with What-If Analysis 118

Optimize a Result with Goal Seek 120

Creating Charts

Create a Chart That Has Visual Appeal 124

Add Chart Details 126

Change the Chart Type 130

Add a Trendline to a Chart 132

Add and Remove Chart Data 134

Add Error Bars 136

Create a Histogram 138

Presenting Worksheets

Format Quickly with Format Painter 142

Insert Shapes into a Worksheet 144

Insert Text Boxes into a Worksheet 146

Insert Photographs into a Worksheet 148

Arrange the Graphics in a Worksheet 150

Insert a Background Image 152

Take a Picture of a Worksheet 154

Protecting, Saving, and Printing

Protect a Worksheet 158

Save a Workbook as a Template 160

Choose a Format when Saving a Workbook 162

Print Multiple Areas of a Worksheet 164

Print Multiple Worksheets from a Workbook 166

chapter 9 Extending Excel

Paste Link into Word or PowerPoint 170

Embed a Worksheet 172

Hyperlink a Worksheet 174

Query a Website 176

Import a Text File 178

Import an Access Database 182

Query an Access Database 184

Reuse a Saved Query 188

Export a Worksheet to Access 190

chapter 10 Customizing Excel

Install Add-Ins 196

Customize the Quick Access Toolbar 198

Work with Multiple Windows 200

Save Time by Creating a Custom View 201

Create a Custom Number Format 202

Automate a Worksheet with Macros 204

Create an Icon to Run a Macro 206

Index 208

Chapter

1

Boosting Efficiency

You can use Microsoft Excel 2007 to work with numbers. In fact, wherever you use numbers — doing taxes, running a small business, maintaining a budget, or anything else — Excel can help make your work easier, quicker, and more accurate.

Excel 2007 provides you with many ways to enter, present, explore, and analyze data. This chapter focuses on ways in which you can boost your efficiency when using Excel. The chapter starts by showing you how to create a range name. Range names make creating formulas easier, because range names are easier to remember than cell addresses. You also learn how to validate your entries, incorporate symbols and special characters in your worksheet, and use the Excel AutoFill feature. The AutoFill

feature enables you to fill a row or column quickly, with a series of values, numbers, dates, or times generated from one or more values you have entered.

You can use grouping and outlining to hide parts of your worksheet, enabling you to focus in on the data in which you are interested, thereby making data analysis easier. When more than one person uses a workbook, comments can be an efficient way to communicate.

Sometimes you may want to double-check the accuracy of your data. This chapter ends by teaching you how you can increase the accuracy of your data entry by letting Excel read back your data to you.

Quick Tips

Name Cells and Ranges..4

Validate with a Validation List..6

Validate with Data Entry Rules 8

Extend a Series with AutoFill...10

Insert Symbols and Special Characters 12

Hide Rows by Grouping and Outlining 14

Add Comments to a Worksheet..16

Let Excel Read Back Data...18

Name Cells and Ranges

In Excel, you can name a cell or range of cells and then use the range name in formulas. Naming makes creating formulas easier, because range names are easier to remember than cell addresses.

You determine the scope of the name by telling Excel whether it applies to the current worksheet or the entire workbook. You can name several ranges at once by using Excel's Create from Selection option. Use the Name Manager to add, edit, or delete named ranges.

Excel range names must be fewer than 255 characters. The first character must be a letter. You cannot use spaces or symbols except for the period and underscore. To learn how to use a named range, see Chapter 2.

NAME A RANGE OF CELLS

① Click and drag to select the cells you want to name.

Alternatively, click a cell with a value to create a named cell.

② Click the Formulas tab.

③ Click Define Name.

The New Name dialog box appears.

④ Type a name for the range.

⑤ Click here and then select the scope of the range.

● The range you selected in step 1 appears here.

⑥ Click OK.

Excel creates a named range.

The defined names are now available when you click Use in Formula.

CREATE NAMED RANGES FROM A SELECTION

① Select the cells you want to include in the range. Include the headings you want to use as the range names.

② Click Create from Selection.

③ Click the location of your range names.

④ Click OK.

The defined names are now available when you click Use in Formula.

● You can click here to move to a named range.

⑤ Click Name Manager.

All range names are available for editing and deleting in the Name Manager.

⑥ Click a name.

⑦ Click Edit.

The Edit Name dialog box appears. You can edit your named range.

TIP

Did You Know?

If you click the Edit button in the Name Manager dialog box, you can change the range name or the cell address to which a named range refers. When creating a formula, if you click and drag to select a group of cells that have a range name, Excel automatically uses the range name instead of the cell address.

Validate with a Validation List

During data entry, a validation list forces anyone using your worksheet to select a value from a drop-down menu rather than type it — and potentially type the wrong information. In this way, validation lists save time and reduce errors.

To create a validation list, type the values you want to include into adjacent cells in a column or row. You may want to name the range. After you have typed your values, use the Data Validation dialog box to assign values to a validation list. Then copy and paste your validation list into the appropriate cells by using the Paste Special Validation option.

CREATE A VALIDATION LIST

1. Click the cell in which you want to create the validation list.

2. Click the Data tab.

3. Click Data Validation.

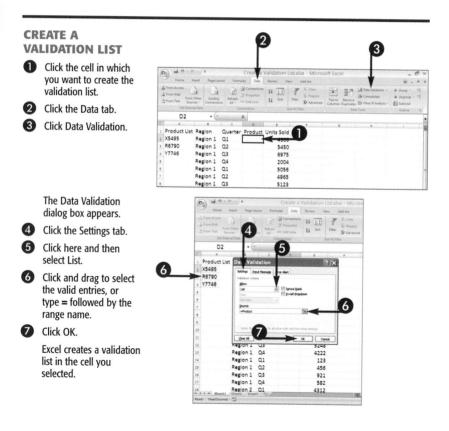

The Data Validation dialog box appears.

4. Click the Settings tab.

5. Click here and then select List.

6. Click and drag to select the valid entries, or type = followed by the range name.

7. Click OK.

Excel creates a validation list in the cell you selected.

PASTE YOUR VALIDATION LIST

1 Click the cell that contains your validation list.

2 Click the Home tab.

3 Click the Copy icon.

4 Select the cells in which you want to place the validation list.

5 Click Paste.

   A menu appears.

6 Click Paste Special.

   The Paste Special dialog box appears.

7 Click to select the Validation option.

8 Click OK.

   Excel places the validation list in the cells you selected.

   When a user makes an entry into the cell, they must pick from the list.

TIP

Remove It!

To remove a validation list, click any cell that contains the validation list you want to remove, click the Home tab, and then click Find and Select. In the menu that appears, click Go To Special. The Go To Special dialog box appears. Click Data validation, click Same, and then click OK. The Go To Special dialog box closes. Click the Data tab and then click the Data Validation icon. The Data Validation dialog box appears. Click the Clear All button and then click OK.

7

Validate with Data Entry Rules

You can use data entry rules to ensure that data entered has the correct format and you can restrict the data entered to whole numbers, decimals, dates, times, or a specific text length. You can also specify whether the values need to be between, not between, equal to, not equal to, greater than, less than, greater than or equal to, or less than or equal to the values you specify.

As with all data validation, you can create an input message that appears when the user enters the cell, as well as an error alert that displays if the user makes an incorrect entry. Error alerts can stop the user, provide a warning, or just provide information.

① Click the cell in which you want to create a data entry rule.

② Click the Data tab.

③ Click Data Validation.

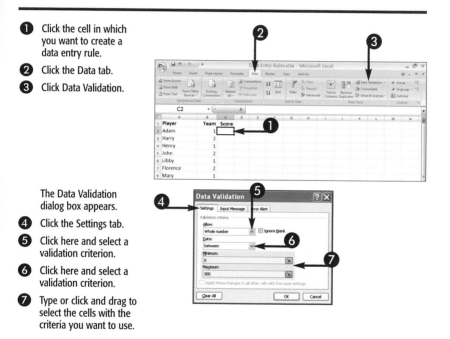

The Data Validation dialog box appears.

④ Click the Settings tab.

⑤ Click here and select a validation criterion.

⑥ Click here and select a validation criterion.

⑦ Type or click and drag to select the cells with the criteria you want to use.

Data Validation ?X

| Settings | Input Message | Error Alert |

☑ Show input message when cell is selected

When cell is selected, show this input message:

Title:

Scores ← **9**

Input message:

Scores must be between 0 and 300. ← **10**

Clear All | OK | Cancel

8 Click the Input Message tab.

9 Type a title.

10 Type an input message.

Data Validation ?X

| Settings | Input Message | Error Alert | ← **11**

☑ Show error alert after invalid data is entered

When user enters invalid data, show this error alert:

Style: **12**

Stop ⌄

Title: **13**

Invalid Scores

14 Error message:

You must enter a score between 0 and 300.

✗

Clear All **15** OK | Cancel

11 Click the Error Alert tab.

12 Click here and select a style.

13 Type a title.

14 Type an error message.

15 Click OK.

Excel creates the data entry rule.

TIP

Important!
After you create your data entry rules, use the steps outlined in the previous section, "Validate with a Validation List," under Paste Your Validation List, to place your data entry rules in the cells in which you want them.

Extend a Series with AutoFill

AutoFill helps you quickly enter data when a data series has an intrinsic order such as days of the week, months of the year, numeric increments of two, and so on.

To use AutoFill, you simply click the Fill handle in the lower-right corner of your selection and drag. When you release the mouse button, Excel fills the cells with values.

After filling the cells, Excel provides a menu icon. You can click the icon to open a menu that enables you to change the fill. Using the menu, you can copy the initial value, fill the series one day at a time, or extend it by weekdays, months, or years, depending on the type of fill you created.

1. Type the initial value for the series you want to create.

2. Select the cell or cells.

3. Click the Fill handle.

4. Drag the desired number of cells and release the mouse.

   Excel fills the cells with a series.

● An icon appears.

5. Click the icon.

   A menu appears.

6. Click Copy Cells.

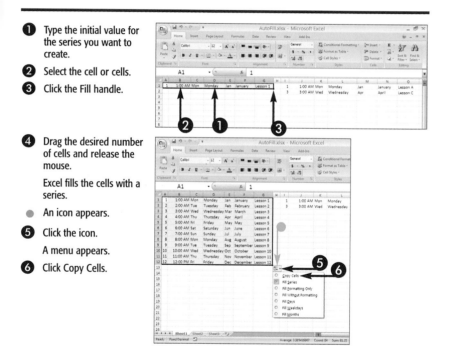

Excel changes the series to a copy of the original cell.

⑦ Type a pattern of entries.

⑧ Repeat steps 2 to 4.

	A	B	C	D	E	F	G	H	I	J	K	L	M	N	O
1	1	1:00 AM	Mon	Monday	Jan	January	Lesson 1		1	1:00 AM	Mon	Monday	Jan	January	Lesson A
2	1	1:00 AM	Mon	Monday	Jan	January	Lesson 1		3	3:00 AM	Wed	Wednesday	Apr	April	Lesson C
3	1	1:00 AM	Mon	Monday	Jan	January	Lesson 1								
4	1	1:00 AM	Mon	Monday	Jan	January	Lesson 1								
5	1	1:00 AM	Mon	Monday	Jan	January	Lesson 1								
6	1	1:00 AM	Mon	Monday	Jan	January	Lesson 1								
7	1	1:00 AM	Mon	Monday	Jan	January	Lesson 1								
8	1	1:00 AM	Mon	Monday	Jan	January	Lesson 1								
9	1	1:00 AM	Mon	Monday	Jan	January	Lesson 1								
10	1	1:00 AM	Mon	Monday	Jan	January	Lesson 1								
11	1	1:00 AM	Mon	Monday	Jan	January	Lesson 1								
12	1	1:00 AM	Mon	Monday	Jan	January	Lesson 1								
13															
14															

Excel fills the cells with the pattern.

	I	J	K	L	M	N	O
1	1	1:00 AM	Mon	Monday	Jan	January	Lesson A
3	3	3:00 AM	Wed	Wednesday	Apr	April	Lesson C
5	5	5:00 AM	Fri	Friday	Jul	July	Lesson A
7	7	7:00 AM	Sun	Sunday	Oct	October	Lesson C
9	9	9:00 AM	Tue	Tuesday	Jan	January	Lesson A
11	11	11:00 AM	Thu	Thursday	Apr	April	Lesson C
13	13	1:00 PM	Sat	Saturday	Jul	July	Lesson A
15	15	3:00 PM	Mon	Monday	Oct	October	Lesson C
17	17	5:00 PM	Wed	Wednesday	Jan	January	Lesson A
19	19	7:00 PM	Fri	Friday	Apr	April	Lesson C
21	21	9:00 PM	Sun	Sunday	Jul	July	Lesson A
23	23	11:00 PM	Tue	Tuesday	Oct	October	Lesson C

TIP

Did You Know?

When you release the mouse button after creating a series, an icon appears. Clicking the icon presents you with a menu of options. Click the Fill Formatting Only option to change the formatting of the filled cells without changing the contents. Click the Fill Without Formatting option to change the contents of the filled cells without changing the formatting. You can extend a series in any direction: up, down, left, or right.

Insert Symbols and Special Characters

In Excel, you are not restricted to the standard numerals, letters, and punctuation marks on your keyboard. You can also select from hundreds of special characters, such as foreign letters and currency characters such as the Euro (€). A smaller set of standard characters, called symbols, is always available as well; they include dashes, hyphens, and quotation marks.

Using symbols and special characters in the same cell with a value such as a number, date, or time usually prevents you from using the value in a formula. If you need to use a symbol in a cell you use in a formula, you should use a number format. If you need to create a custom number format, see Chapter 10.

ADD A SYMBOL

① Click the cell in which you want to insert a symbol.

② Click the Insert tab.

③ Click the Symbol icon.

The Symbol dialog box appears.

④ Locate the symbol you want, and click it.

⑤ Click Insert.

● The symbol appears in the cell.

⑥ Click Close.

The Symbol dialog box closes.

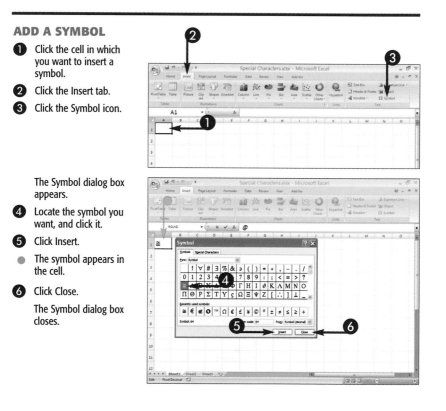

12

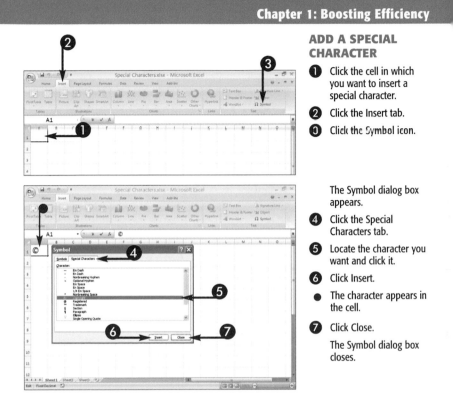

ADD A SPECIAL CHARACTER

1. Click the cell in which you want to insert a special character.

2. Click the Insert tab.

3. Click the Symbol icon.

The Symbol dialog box appears.

4. Click the Special Characters tab.

5. Locate the character you want and click it.

6. Click Insert.

● The character appears in the cell.

7. Click Close.

The Symbol dialog box closes.

TIP

Did You Know?

In Excel, entries are numbers, dates, times, letters, or special characters. You can only use numbers, dates, and times in numeric calculations. Excel treats letters and special characters as blanks, or zeroes. To have the currency symbol appear with a value, as in $400, and use the cell value in a calculation, you must apply a currency, accounting, or custom format.

Hide Rows by Grouping and Outlining

You can use the Excel grouping and outlining feature to hide sets of columns and/or rows. For example, you can hide the details relating to weekly sales so you can compare monthly sales. Your outlines can include up to eight levels of detail.

Outlining a set of rows or columns creates a clickable button on the far left or top of the worksheet. The button displays either a minus sign or a plus sign. You click the minus sign to hide rows or columns, and the plus sign to display them again. Adjacent to the button is a solid vertical line that indicates, by its length, the scope of the hidden details, and the approximate number of rows or columns Excel has hidden.

---

① Click and drag to select the rows or columns to hide.

② Click the Data tab.

③ Click Group.

You can also select the rows or columns and then press Shift+Alt+Right Arrow.

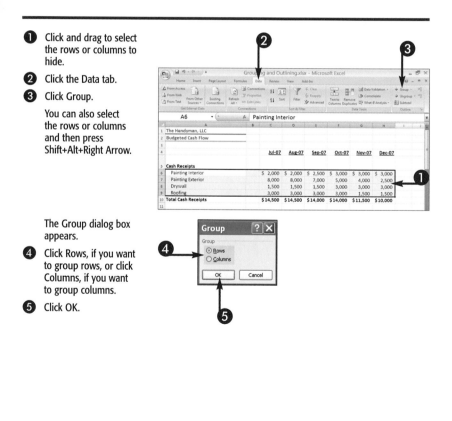

The Group dialog box appears.

④ Click Rows, if you want to group rows, or click Columns, if you want to group columns.

⑤ Click OK.

● Excel creates a new left margin with a minus sign.

6 To hide the rows, click the minus sign.

The rows disappear, and the plus sign replaces the minus sign.

7 Click the plus sign, to display the rows again.

Apply It!

If you want to remove an outline, display the outline by clicking the plus sign. Click and drag to select the rows or columns you want to remove from the outline. Click the Data tab and then click Ungroup. The Ungroup dialog box appears. Click Rows to ungroup rows or click Columns to ungroup columns.

Add Comments to a Worksheet

If someone else maintains your worksheet, or others use it in a workgroup, your comments can provide useful information. Excel associates comments with individual cells and indicates their presence with a tiny red triangle in the cell's upper-right corner.

You can view an individual comment by clicking the cell or passing your cursor over it. You can view all comments in a worksheet by clicking the Review tab and then clicking Show All Comments.

When you track your changes, Excel automatically generates a comment every time you copy or change a cell. The comment records what was changed in the cell, who made the change, and the time and date of the change. To learn more about tracking changes, see Chapter 3.

ADD A COMMENT

1 Click in the cell to which you want to add a comment.

2 Click the Review tab.

3 Click New Comment.

A comment box appears.

● A tiny red triangle appears in the upper-right corner of the cell.

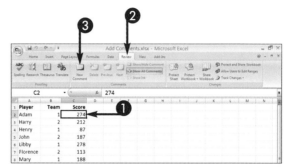

4 Type your comment.

To apply bold and other formatting effects as you type, select the text, right-click, click Format Comment, and then make the changes you want.

● Click inside the cell in which you entered your comment box and click Show/Hide Comment to hide your comment.

Move the cursor over the cell to display your comment again.

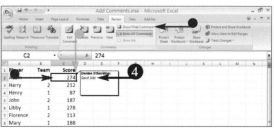

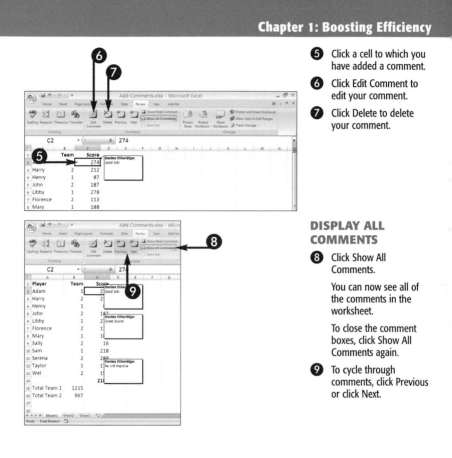

⑤ Click a cell to which you have added a comment.

⑥ Click Edit Comment to edit your comment.

⑦ Click Delete to delete your comment.

DISPLAY ALL COMMENTS

⑧ Click Show All Comments.

You can now see all of the comments in the worksheet.

To close the comment boxes, click Show All Comments again.

⑨ To cycle through comments, click Previous or click Next.

TIP

Did You Know?

To set the name that displays when you enter a comment, click the Microsoft Office button (🔲), and then click Excel Options. The Excel Options dialog box appears. Click Popular and then type the name you want to appear in the comment box in the User name field.

Let Excel Read Back Data

If you have a large amount of data to enter, you may want to check the accuracy by having the data read back. You can click an icon to have Microsoft Excel read your data. You can have Excel read across the first row and then move to the next row, or down the first column and then move to the next column. You can also have Excel read data as you enter it.

Before Excel can read your data, you must add the following icons to the Quick Access toolbar: Speak Cells, Speak Cells — Stop Speaking Cells, Speak Cells by Columns, Speak Cells by Rows, Speak Cells on Enter. To learn how to add icons to the Quick Access toolbar, see Chapter 10.

READ CELLS

① Click and drag to select the cells you want Excel to read.

② Click either the Speak by Columns or the Speak by Rows icon.

● Click Speak by Columns if you want Excel to read down the columns.

● Click Speak by Rows if you want Excel to read across the rows.

③ Click the Speak Cells icon.

Excel reads the cells.

● To stop the reading of cells, click the Speak Cells – Stop Speaking Cells icon.

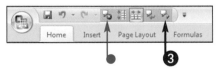

C8 ▾ f_x 18173

	A	B	C	D	E
1	Product Line	Projected Sales	Actual Sales		
2	Dolls	20000	19562		
3	Trucks	30200	31248		
4	Balls	15000	14279		
5	Games	75000	123000		
6	Puzzles	5000	2187		
7	Candy	23000	21569		
8	Bikes	22000	18173		
9					

SPEAK CELLS ON ENTER

④ Click the Speak on Enter icon.

Excel says, "Cells will now be spoken on Enter."

⑤ Enter data into your worksheet.

Excel reads the data as you enter it.

⑥ Click the Speak on Enter icon again.

Excel says, "Turn off Speak on Enter."

Excel stops reading the data as you enter it.

TIP

Important!
To have Excel read your data, you must have speakers attached to your computer and you must set the Speech, Sound and Audio Devices option in the Control Panel properly. Click the Start button, click Settings, and then click Control Panel to check device settings.

Working with Formulas and Functions

Excel provides you with tools for storing numbers and other kinds of information. However, the real power of Excel comes from manipulating all of this information. There are more than 300 functions built into Excel. They enable you to perform tasks of every kind, from adding numbers to calculating the internal rate of return for an investment.

You can think of a function as a black box. You put your information into the box, and out come the results. Each bit of information you provide is called an argument. Excel's Function Wizard provides guidance for every function and for every argument. A formula consists of an equal sign, one or more functions, their arguments, operators such as the division and multiplication symbols, and any other values required to get your results.

Many Excel functions do special-purpose financial, statistical, engineering, and mathematical calculations. The Function Wizard arranges functions in categories for easy access. For example, the Payment (PMT) function in the Financial category, enables you to determine an optimal loan payment for a given principal, interest rate, and length of loan.

This chapter introduces useful techniques that make creating formulas and functions easier, including the Function Wizard and the Excel calculator. You can also find tips for working more efficiently with functions by naming cells and creating constants. Finally, you can find tips for functions such as IF, and special-purpose functions such as PMT and Internal Rate of Return (IRR).

Calculate with the Function Wizard..22

Define a Constant..24

Create Formulas That Include Names..26

Figure Out Loan Terms 28

Determine the Internal Rate of Return 30

Determine the Nth Largest Value..32

Create a Conditional Formula 34

Calculate a Conditional Sum 36

Add a Calculator..38

Find Products and Square Roots 40

Perform Time Calculations 42

Perform Date Calculations 44

Excel's Function Wizard simplifies the use of functions. You can take advantage of the wizard for every one of Excel's functions. For example, one simple but useful function, ROUND, rounds off values to the number of places you specify.

You can access the Function Wizard in several ways. The first involves selecting a cell where the result is to appear and then clicking the Insert Function icon. A second way makes sense when you know the name of your function. Type an equal sign and the beginning of the function name. In the list of functions that appears, double-click the function you want and then click the Insert Function icon. Both methods bring up the Function Arguments dialog box.

① Type your data into your worksheet.

This example uses the ROUND function, which takes two arguments, one indicating the number to be rounded and the other indicating the number of digits to which the number is to be rounded.

② Click the cell in which you want the results to appear.

③ Click the Insert Function icon.

The Insert Function dialog box appears.

④ Click here and select All to list all of the functions.

⑤ Double-click the function you want to use.

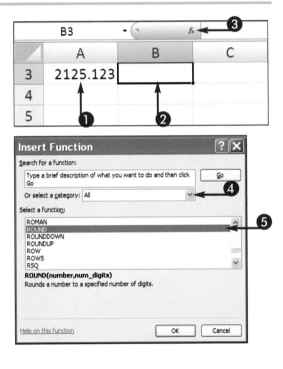

Function Arguments ? X

ROUND

| Number | A3 | [icon] | = 2125.123 |
| Num_digits | -2 | [icon] | = -2 |

= 2100

Rounds a number to a specified number of digits.

Num_digits is the number of digits to which you want to round.
Negative rounds to the left of the decimal point; zero to
the nearest integer.

Formula result = 2100

Help on this function   **⑦** → OK   Cancel

| | B3 | ▾ | fx | =ROUND(A3,-2) |

	A	B	C	D
3	2125.123	2100 ◄		
4				
5				
6				

The Function Arguments
dialog box appears.

⑥ Click the cells or type the
values requested in each
field.

● For this example, click
the cell containing the
value you entered in
step 1.

● Type the number of
decimal places to which
you want to round. A
negative number refers
to decimal places to the
left of the decimal point.

● The results show here.

⑦ Click OK.

● The result appears in the
cell.

TIP

Did You Know?
If you do not know which function you want to use, type a question
in the Search for a function field in the Insert Function dialog box. For
help with the function itself, click the Help on this function link in the
Function Arguments dialog box.

You can use a constant whenever you want to apply the same value in different contexts. With constants, you refer to a value by simply using the constant's name.

You can use constants in many applications. For example, a sales tax rate is a familiar constant that, when multiplied by the subtotal on an invoice, results in the tax owed.

To create a constant, define its name by using the New Name dialog box, the same dialog box you use to name ranges and formulas. You can define the scope of the constant by limiting its use to a specific worksheet or by making it available to the entire workbook. To use a constant, simply enter the name you defined.

DEFINE A CONSTANT

① Click the Formulas tab.

② Click Define Name.

The New Name dialog box appears.

③ Type a name for the constant.

④ Click here and select the scope of the constant.

⑤ Type = followed by the constant's value.

⑥ Click OK.

You can now use the constant.

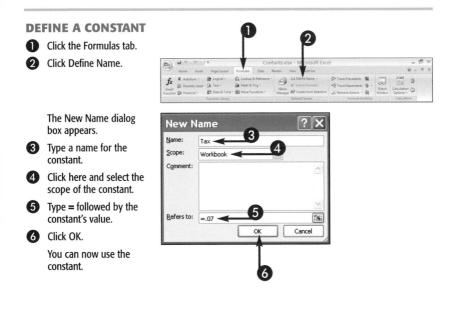

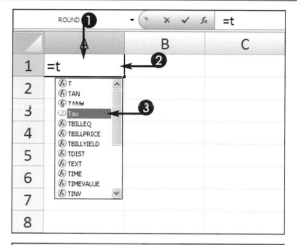

DISPLAY A CONSTANT

① Click a cell.

② Type = followed by the first letter or letters of the constant's name.

A menu appears.

Note: *If you do not know the constant's name, click the Formulas tab, and then click Use in Formula. A menu appears. Click the name and then press Enter.*

③ Double-click the name of the constant.

④ Press Enter.

● The constant's value appears in the cell.

Note: *To use named constants and ranges in formulas, see section "Create Formulas That Include Names."*

TIP

Did You Know?

You can use Excel's Name Manager feature to rename, edit, or delete named ranges and constant values. On the Formulas tab, click Name Manager. The Name Manager dialog box appears. Double-click the name you want to edit. The Edit Name dialog box appears. Make the changes you want and then click OK. To delete a constant, click the name in the Name Manager dialog box and then click Delete.

Create Formulas That Include Names

Constructing formulas can be complicated, especially when you use several functions in the same formula or when multiple arguments are required in a single function. A named constant is a name you create that refers to a single, frequently used value. A named range is a name you assign to a group of related cells. Using named constants and named ranges can make creating formulas and functions easier by enabling you to use names that clearly identify a value or range of values.

To insert a name into a function, or use it in a formula or as a function's argument, you must access it by clicking the Use in Formula button, or select it from the Function AutoComplete list.

USE A RANGE NAME IN A FORMULA

① Place the cursor in the formula.

② Type the name of the range.

● As you type, a list of possible values appears. Double-click a value to place it in the formula.

③ Press Enter.

● The cell displays the result.

USE A CONSTANT IN A FORMULA

Note: Use this technique if you forget the name of a constant or range.

① Begin typing your formula.

② Click the Formulas tab.

③ Click Use in Formula.

A menu appears.

④ Click the constant name you want to use.

If necessary, continue typing the formula, and press Enter when you finish.

⑤ Press Enter.

● Excel feeds the selected constant into the formula and then displays a result based on it.

Did You Know?

You can create several named constants at the same time. Simply create two adjacent columns, one listing names and the other listing the values — for example, state names and state sales tax rates. Select both columns. Click the Formulas tab and then click Create from Selection. In the Create Names from Selection dialog box that appears, click a check box to indicate which column or row to use for the name. Click OK.

Figure Out Loan Terms

You can use Excel's Payment function (PMT) when buying a house or car. This function enables you to compare loan terms and make an objective decision, based on factors such as the amount of the monthly payment.

The PMT function takes three required arguments. For Rate, enter an annual interest rate such as 5 percent and then type .05 divided by 12 to calculate the monthly rate. For Nper, the number of periods, enter the number of loan periods for the loan you are seeking. For PV, present value, enter the amount of the loan. The monthly payment appears surrounded by parentheses, signifying that the number is negative, or a cash outflow.

① Type the principal (the PV), interest rate, and number of periods.

② Click the cell in which you want the results to appear.

③ Click the Insert Function icon.

	A	B	C	D
	B4		f_x ← ③	
1	Principal	120000		
2	Interest	0.05 ← ①		
3	Number of Months	180		
4	Monthly Payments	← ②		
5				
6				

The Insert Function dialog box appears.

④ Click here and select Financial.

⑤ Double-click PMT.

Insert Function

Search for a function:

Type a brief description of what you want to do and then click Go   [Go]

Or select a category: Financial ← ④

Select a function:

ODDLPRICE
ODDLYIELD
PMT ← ⑤
PPMT
PRICE
PRICEDISC
PRICEMAT

PMT(rate,nper,pv,fv,type)
Calculates the payment for a loan based on constant payments and a constant interest rate.

Help on this function   [OK]   [Cancel]

The Function Arguments dialog box appears for the PMT function.

⑥ Click the cell with the interest rate.

⑦ Divide the interest rate by the number of periods per year; for example, type **12**.

⑧ Click the cell with the number of periods.

⑨ In the Pv field, click the cell with the principal.

⑩ Click OK.

● The result appears in the cell.

The result shows the amount of a single loan payment.

You can repeat steps 1 to 10 for other combinations of the three variables.

	A	B	C	D	E	F
1	Principal	120000				
2	Interest	0.05				
3	Number of Months	180				
4	Monthly Payments	($948.95)				
5						
6						

B4 — fx =PMT(B2/12,B3,B1)

TIP

Did You Know?

Excel's Goal Seeking feature enables you to calculate payments. For example, you can set up a problem so that you specify a goal, such as payments of less than $1,100 per month, and have Excel vary a single value to reach the goal. The limitation is that you can vary only one value at a time. See Chapter 5 for more information on Goal Seek.

Determine the Internal Rate of Return

You can use Excel's Internal Rate of Return (IRR) function to calculate the rate of return on an investment. When using the IRR function, the cash flows do not have to be equal, but they must occur at regular intervals. As an example, you may make a loan of $6,607 on January 1, year 1. You receive payments every January 1 for four succeeding years. You can use the IRR function to determine the interest rate you receive on the loan.

Your loan of $6,607 is a cash outflow, so you enter it as a negative number. Each payment is a cash inflow, so you enter them as positive numbers. When using the IRR function, you must enter at least one positive and one negative number.

CALCULATE INTERNAL RATE OF RETURN

① Type the series of projected cash flows into a worksheet.

② Click the cell in which you want the results to appear.

③ Click the Insert Function icon.

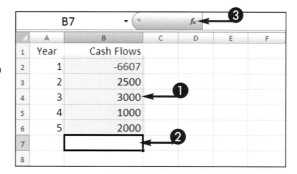

The Insert Function dialog box appears.

④ Type **IRR**.

⑤ Click Go.

The IRR function appears in the Select a function box.

⑥ Double-click IRR.

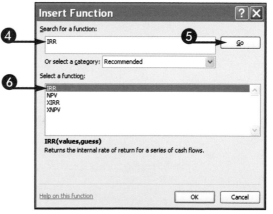

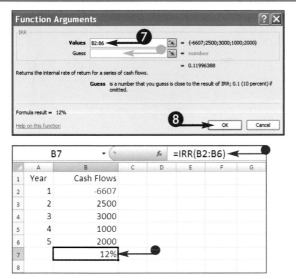

The Function Arguments dialog box for IRR appears.

7 Click and drag or type the range for the cash-flow values entered in step 1.

● Optionally, you can provide an estimated rate of return just to get Excel started.

8 Click OK.

● The cell with the formula displays the results of the calculations as a percent with no decimal places.

Repeat steps 1 to 8 for each set of anticipated future cash flows.

Caution!
Excel's IRR function has strict assumptions. Cash flows must be regularly timed and take place at the same point within the payment period. IRR may perform less reliably for inconsistent payments, a mix of positive and negative flows, and variable interest rates.

Sometimes you want to identify and characterize the top values in any series, such as the runs batted in for the top three hitters in the Major Leagues.

The LARGE function evaluates a series of numbers and determines the highest value, second highest, or nth-highest value

in the series, with n being a value's rank order. LARGE takes two arguments: the range of cells you want to evaluate and the rank order of the value you are seeking, with 1 being the highest, 2 the next highest, and so on. The result of LARGE is the value you requested.

 ① Type the values from which you want to identify the highest number, the second highest, or another value.

② Click the cell in which you want the results to appear.

③ Click the Insert Function icon.

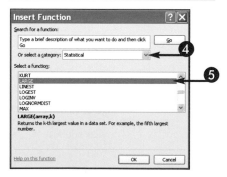

The Insert Function dialog box appears.

④ Click here and select Statistical.

⑤ Double-click LARGE.

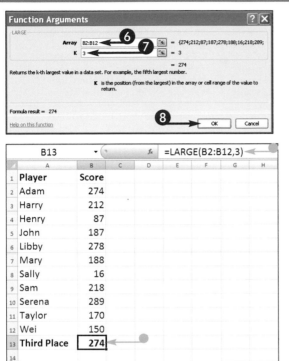

The Function Arguments dialog box for the LARGE function appears.

6 Click and drag to select or type the range for the cells you want to evaluate.

7 Type a number indicating what you are seeking (1 for highest, 2 for second highest, 3 for third highest, and so on).

8 Click OK.

● The cell displays the value you requested.

If k in step 7 is greater than the number of cells, a #NUM error appears in the cell instead.

Did You Know?

Other useful functions work much like the LARGE function. SMALL evaluates a range of values and returns a number. For example, if you enter 1 as the k value, it returns the lowest number, 2 for next lowest, and so on. The MIN and MAX functions return the lowest and highest values in a series, respectively. They take one argument: a range of cell values.

Create a Conditional Formula

With a conditional formula, you can perform calculations on numbers that meet a certain condition. For example, you can find the highest score for a particular team from a list that consists of several teams.

A conditional formula uses at least two functions. The first function, IF, defines the condition, or test, such as players on Team 1. To create the condition, you use comparison operators, such as greater than (>), greater than or equal to (>=), less than (<), or equal to (=).

The second function in a conditional formula performs a calculation on numbers that meet the condition. Excel carries out the IF function first and then calculates the values that meet the condition defined in the IF function.

① Type your data into your worksheet.

② Click the cell in which you want your results to appear.

③ Click the Insert Function icon.

	B	C	D	E	F	G	H
1	Player	Team	Score				
2	Adam	1	274				
3	Harry	2	212				
4	Henry	1	87				
5	John	2	187				
6	Libby	1	278				
7	Florence	2	113				
8	Mary	1	188				
9	Sally	2	16				
10	Sam	1	218				
11	Serena	2	289				
12	Taylor	1	170				
13	Wei	2	150				
14							
15	Totals						
16	High Score Team 1	278					
17	High Score Team 2						
18							

The Insert Function dialog box appears.

④ Click here and select All.

⑤ Double-click the function on which you want to base your conditional function.

● This example uses MAX, which finds the highest value in a list.

Insert Function

Search for a function:

Type a brief description of what you want to do and then click Go — Go

Or select a category: All

Select a function:

MATCH
MAX
MAXA
MDETERM
MDURATION
MEDIAN
MID

MAX(number1,number2,...)
Returns the largest value in a set of values. Ignores logical values and text.

Help on this function — OK Cancel

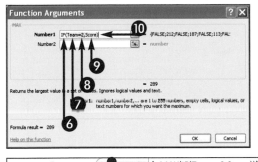

The Function Arguments
dialog box for the MAX
function appears.

⑥ Type **IF(**.

⑦ Type the range or range
name for the series you
want to evaluate.

⑧ Type a comparison
operator, the condition,
and then a comma.

⑨ Type the range or range
name for the series that
you want to calculate.

⑩ Type **)**.

⑪ Press Ctrl+Shift+Enter.

● The result appears in the
cell with the formula.

	B	C	D	E	F	G	H	I
1	Player	Team	Score					
2	Adam	1	274					
3	Harry	2	212					
4	Henry	1	87					
5	John	2	187					
6	Libby	1	278					
7	Florence	2	113					
8	Mary	1	188					
9	Sally	2	16					
10	Sam	1	218					
11	Serena	2	289					
12	Taylor	1	170					
13	Wei	2	150					
14								
15	Totals							
16	High Score Team 1	278						
17	High Score Team 2	289						
18								

C17 — {=MAX(IF(Team=2,Score))}

Important!

IF is an array function. It compares every number in a series to a
condition and keeps track of the numbers that meet the condition. To
create an array function, you press Ctrl+Shift+Enter instead of the Enter
key to complete your function. You must surround arrays with curly
braces ({ }). Excel enters the braces automatically when you press
Ctrl+Shift+Enter, but not when you press Enter.

Calculate a Conditional Sum

You can use conditional sums to identify and sum investments whose growth exceeds a certain rate, or other useful quantities. The SUMIF function combines the SUM and IF functions into one easy-to-use function.

SUMIF takes three arguments: a range of numbers, the condition you want to apply to the numbers, and the range to which the condition applies. Excel adds values that meet the condition together. For example, you can create a function that evaluates a list to determine the team a person is on, and for all persons on Team 1 it can add the scores. The third argument, the range to which the condition applies, is optional. If you exclude it, Excel sums the range you specify in the first argument.

---

① Create a list of values to sum conditionally.

Excel tests each value in the list to determine whether it meets the condition you specify. If it does, Excel adds it to other values that meet the condition.

② Click the cell in which you want the results to appear.

③ Click the Insert Function icon.

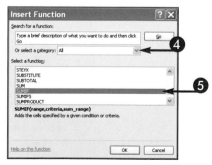

The Insert Function dialog box appears.

④ Click here and select All.

⑤ Double-click SUMIF.

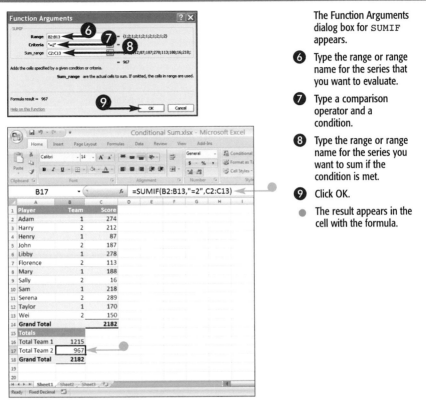

The Function Arguments dialog box for SUMIF appears.

⑥ Type the range or range name for the series that you want to evaluate.

⑦ Type a comparison operator and a condition.

⑧ Type the range or range name for the series you want to sum if the condition is met.

⑨ Click OK.

● The result appears in the cell with the formula.

Often you may want to do quick calculations without using a formula or function. In Excel, you can place a calculator on the Quick Access toolbar so that it is always available.

You can use the calculator as you would any electronic calculator. You simply click a number, choose an operator, and then click another number. You then click the

Equals key to get a result. You can use MC to remember a value, MR to recall it, and MS to clear memory.

Statistical and mathematical functions are available in the calculator's scientific view. You can transfer a value from the calculator to Excel by displaying it, copying it, and then pasting it into a cell.

ADD THE CALCULATOR

1 Click here.

2 Click More Commands.

The Customize the Quick Access Toolbar dialog box appears.

3 Click here and select Commands Not in the Ribbon.

4 Click Calculator.

5 Click Add.

● Excel adds the calculator to the list on the right.

6 Click OK.

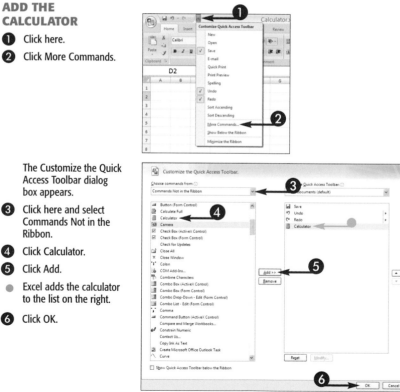

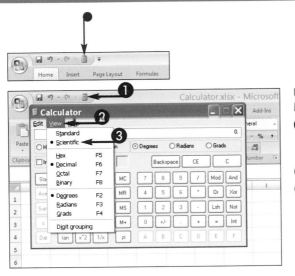

● The Calculator icon appears on the Quick Access toolbar, and is ready to use.

USE THE SCIENTIFIC MODE

① Click the Calculator icon.

The Calculator window appears.

② Click View.

③ Click Scientific.

The scientific calculator is now available to use.

Apply It!

To calculate an average, switch to the scientific view and enter the first number you want to average. Click the Sta button to bring up the Statistics Box dialog box. Click the Dat button. Back in the calculator, click another value to average and click the Dat button. Keep entering data and clicking the Dat button until you have entered all of the values. Click the Ave button to find the average.

Find Products and Square Roots

Using the PRODUCT function, you can multiply two or more numbers, and using the SQRT function, you can find the square root of a number.

Excel can only calculate the square roots of positive numbers. If a negative number is the argument, as in SQRT(-1), Excel returns #NUM in the cell.

You can use PRODUCT or SQRT by entering the values you want to use in the function into the worksheet. If you do not want the values to appear in the worksheet, you must start by clicking the cell where the result is to appear and typing an equal sign, the function name (PRODUCT or SQRT), and parentheses. You can click the Insert Function icon (fx) to enter your values for the formula.

CALCULATE A PRODUCT

1. Type the values you want to multiply.

2. Click the cell in which you want the results to appear.

3. Type **=product(** in the cell.

   As you begin to type, the Function Auto complete list appears. Double-click an option to select it.

4. Click the Insert Function icon.

   The Function Arguments dialog box for the PRODUCT function appears.

5. Click or type the cell address or the first value you want to multiply.

6. Click or type the cell address of the second value you want to multiply.

7. Click OK.

   The product appears in the cell that you clicked in step 2.

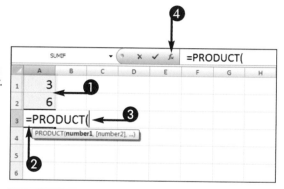

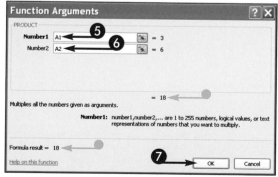

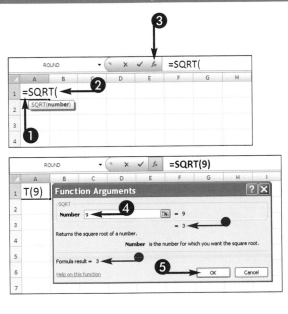

CALCULATE A SQUARE ROOT

① Click the cell in which you want the results to appear.

② Type **=SQRT(** in the formula bar or in the cell in which you want the result to appear.

As you begin to type, the Function Auto complete list appears. Double-click an option to select it.

③ Click the Insert Function icon.

The Function Arguments dialog box for SQRT appears.

④ Type the value for which you want the square root.

Optionally, you can click a cell containing the value.

● The Insert Function dialog box displays the interim answer.

⑤ Click OK.

The square root appears in the cell.

TIP

Did You Know?

Each argument in the PRODUCT function can have more than one value, for example, 1, 2, and 3. These values are represented as an array, a series of numbers enclosed in curly braces, such as {1,2,3}. Each value in the array is multiplied, so the product of {1,2,3} is 6. Excel can multiply array values by each other. Keep in mind that each value in the array has to be a number.

You can find the number of hours worked between two times or the number of days between two dates. Excel converts dates and times into a serial value that it can add, subtract, and then convert back to a recognizable date or time.

Excel calculates a date's serial value as the number of days after January 1, 1900. Excel calculates a time's serial value in units of ⅒ of a second. Every time can be represented as a serial value between 0 and 1.

A date and time consists of the date to the left of the decimal and a time to the right. For example, the date and time of August 25, 2005, at 5:46 PM has a serial value of 38589.74028.

FIND THE DIFFERENCE BETWEEN TWO TIMES

1 Type the first time in a cell.

Note: If you do not include AM or PM, Excel defaults to AM If you want p.m., you must type in PM.

2 Type the second time in a cell.

3 Click the cell in which you want the results to appear.

4 Type =.

5 Click the cell with the later time.

6 Type −.

7 Click the cell with the earlier time.

8 Press Enter.

	C2		
	A	B	C	D
1	Departure Time	Arrival Time	Travel Time (hours: min)	
2	2:20 AM	11:15 PM		
3	6:35 AM	7:45 AM		1:10
4	10:22 AM	12:30 PM		2:08
5	11:55 AM	4:26 PM		4:31
6	11:30 PM	3:00 AM		3:30
7				

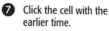

	ROUND		=B2-A2
	A	B	C	D
1	Departure Time	Arrival Time	Travel Time (hours: min)	
2	2:20 AM	11:15 PM	=B2-A2	
3	6:35 AM	7:45 AM	1:10	
4	10:22 AM	12:30 PM	2:08	
5	11:55 AM	4:26 PM	4:31	
6	11:30 PM	3:00 AM		
7				

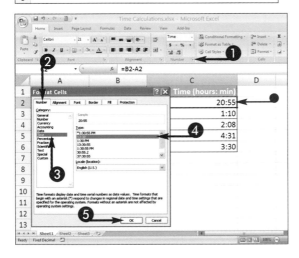

● The result may appear as a serial value.

CONVERT A SERIAL VALUE TO A TIME

① Click the Number group launcher.

The Format Cells dialog box appears.

② Click the Number tab.

③ Click Time.

④ Click a format type.

The 13:30 format displays hours:minutes.

⑤ Click OK.

● The cell now displays the number of hours and minutes between the two times.

TIP

Did You Know?

In subtracting times that cross midnight, such as 11 p.m. to 2 a.m., you need a programming function called modulus, or MOD. The formula is =MOD(later time – earlier time, 1). Thanks to John Walkenbach's *Excel Bible* (Wiley Publishing) for this tip.

The NETWORKDAY function enables you to find the number of workdays between two dates. Like other Excel functions, Date and Time functions make use of the Function Wizard.

The NETWORKDAY function's arguments include a start date, an end date, and optionally, any intervening holidays that automatically reduce the number of

workdays between the two dates. Excel automatically deducts the number of weekend dates.

Excel can perform date arithmetic on any date after January 1, 1900. If you use dates before then, Excel treats them as text and does not perform a calculation on them. Instead, it gives you a #VALUE! error.

FIND NUMBER OF DAYS BETWEEN TWO DATES

① Type the start date.

② Type the end date.

● If you want the calculation to consider holidays, type the dates of holidays between the start and end dates.

③ Click the field in which you want the result to appear.

④ Click the Insert Function icon.

The Insert Function dialog box appears.

⑤ Click here and select Date & Time.

⑥ Double-click NETWORKDAYS.

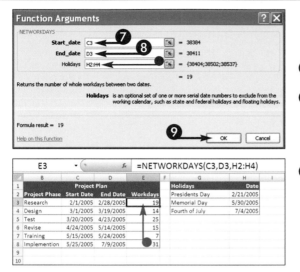

The Function Arguments dialog box for the NETWORKDAYS function appears.

⑦ Click the cell containing the start date.

⑧ Click the cell containing the end date.

● Optionally, click and drag the range of holidays.

⑨ Click OK.

● The cell with the formula displays the net workdays between the two dates.

Did You Know?

In Excel you can enter the current date simply by clicking in the cell in which you want the date to appear, and pressing Ctrl+; at the same time.

Copying, Formatting, and More

If you have used Word, you know that copying text for use in another document or application enables you to reuse material and minimize retyping and errors. Copying data in Excel is similar: You simply select the data you want to copy and click the Copy icon in the Ribbon. Then click the cell in which you want to place the data, and click the Paste icon.

However, copying can be both more involved and more powerful in Excel because in Excel so many elements can occupy a cell: values, functions, formulas, formats, styles, and more. You can copy any of these elements between cells, worksheets, workbooks, and even applications. You can copy one value at a time, such as a specific number or specific bit of text, or many

consecutively arranged values at the same time, such as a range.

Excel makes use of the copy features built into Windows as well as those built into Office 2007. You can store as many as 24 different items on the Office Clipboard for pasting into Excel and other Office applications.

In this chapter, you learn how to use the Office Clipboard. You also learn how to convert a row into a column, to copy styles from one worksheet to another, to copy formulas from one cell to another, to change text to numbers, and much more. If you share your workbooks with others, you will also find useful information on keeping track of changes.

Quick Tips

Check Formulas for Errors 48

Change Text to Numbers and Then Calculate 50

Convert a Row to a Column 52

Copy with the Office Clipboard 54

Specify How to Paste with Paste Special...56

Create Your Own Style 60

Copy Styles to Another Workbook 62

Conditionally Format a Worksheet 64

Track Changes While Editing 68

Consolidate Worksheets 70

You can nest a formula within another formula. Because there are so many intermediate steps when you nest formulas, determining the accuracy of your results may be difficult. You can use the Evaluate Formula dialog box to check the result of intermediate calculations.

The Evaluate Formula dialog box steps you through the calculation one expression at a time so that you can see how Excel evaluates each argument. Click the Evaluate Formula button to begin the process. Excel underlines individual expressions. You can click the Evaluate button to see the results of an expression.

If you based the reference on another formula, you can click the Step In button to display the formula. Click the Step Out button to return to the reference.

① Click the cell that contains the formula.

② Click the Formulas tab.

③ Click the Evaluate Formula icon.

The Evaluate Formula dialog box appears.

④ Click Evaluate.

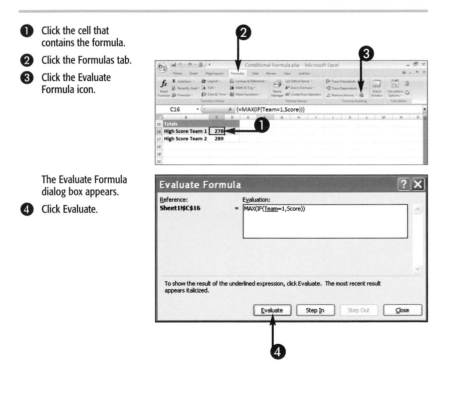

Evaluate Formula [?] [X]

Reference:
Sheet1!$C$16

Evaluation:
= MAX(IF({*TRUE;FALSE;TRUE;FALSE;TRUE;FALSE;TRUE;FALSE;* *TRUE;FALSE;TRUE;FALSE*},Score))

To show the result of the underlined expression, click Evaluate. The most recent result appears italicized.

5 ➤ Evaluate | Step In | Step Out | Close

Evaluate Formula [?] [X]

Reference:
Sheet1!$C$16

Evaluation:
= *278*

To show the result of the underlined expression, click Evaluate. The most recent result appears italicized.

Restart | Step In | Step Out | Close

5 Continue clicking Evaluate to review each expression.

● Click Step In to review the results of an expression.

● Click Step Out to return to the expression.

● When Excel reaches the end of the formula, it displays the results.

● Click Restart to evaluate the formula again.

● Click Close to close the dialog box.

TIP

Did You Know?

The #### error occurs when a cell is not wide enough or when you use a negative date or time. The #DIV/0 error occurs when you try to divide by zero. The #N/A error occurs when a value is not available to your function. The #VALUE error occurs when you use the wrong type of argument or operand.

Change Text to Numbers and Then Calculate

You can use formulas to perform complex calculations quickly and accurately using numbers, dates, or times. Sometimes, however, your numbers look like numbers but are, in fact, text characters. If a number is left-aligned in a cell, it is probably text; true numbers are right-aligned, by default.

When you include text in a complex calculation, it results in an error. You can address this problem in several ways. You can use the Format Cells dialog box to reformat the text cells to numbers, but this method does not always work. A more reliable technique is to multiply each numeral by one.

Note: *These left-aligned numbers are actually text. In Excel, the default position for numbers is the right side of the cell.*

- In this example, you are trying to calculate an average but you cannot because Excel sees the divisor as a zero.

C6		f_x =AVERAGE(C2:C5)				
	A	B	C	D	E	F	G
1	**ID**	**Products**	**Price**	**Units**			
2	1	Combs	3.99	250			
3	2	Brushes	2.99	300			
4	3	Bands	5.99	125			
5	4	Hairspray	3.99	200			
6			#DIV/0!				
7							

1 Type **1** into any neighboring cell.

2 Click the Home tab.

3 Click Copy.

Excel copies the contents of the cell to the Office Clipboard.

Text to Number.xlsx - Micr

Home   Insert   Page Layout   Formulas   Data   Review   View   Add-Ins

F3		f_x 1				
	A	B	C	D	E	F	G
1	**ID**	**Products**	**Price**	**Units**			
2	1	Combs	3.99	250			
3	2	Brushes	2.99	300			1
4	3	Bands	5.99	125			
5	4	Hairspray	3.99	200			
6			#DIV/0!				
7							

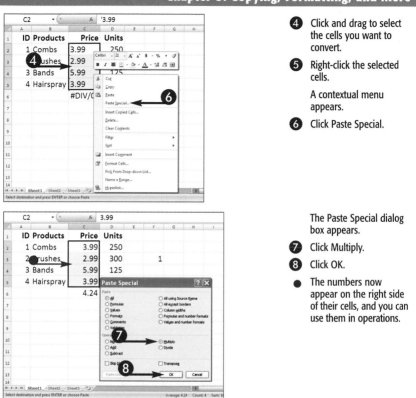

④ Click and drag to select the cells you want to convert.

⑤ Right-click the selected cells.

A contextual menu appears.

⑥ Click Paste Special.

The Paste Special dialog box appears.

⑦ Click Multiply.

⑧ Click OK.

● The numbers now appear on the right side of their cells, and you can use them in operations.

When you create a worksheet, Excel gives you flexibility when working with rows and columns. At any time, you can insert new rows or columns, delete rows or columns, and move entire rows or columns while retaining most of their properties. Sometimes, however, you may want to transpose a row into a column — or vice versa.

With Excel, you can transpose the contents of a row into a column and vice versa by using the Paste Special dialog box. To ensure that you have space for new worksheet data, you can place the transposed columns or rows on a different worksheet or in a new workbook.

---

① Click and drag to select the cells you want to transpose.

Note: Make sure that a series of blank cells is available to accommodate the copied data.

② Click the Home tab.

③ Click the Copy icon.

④ Click to select the first cell in the new column or row.

Note: Excel removes existing data by copying over it.

⑤ Click the Home tab.

⑥ Click Paste.

A menu appears.

⑦ Click Paste Special.

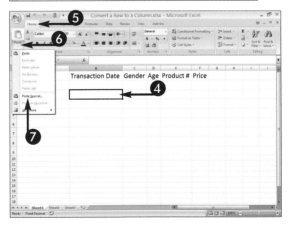

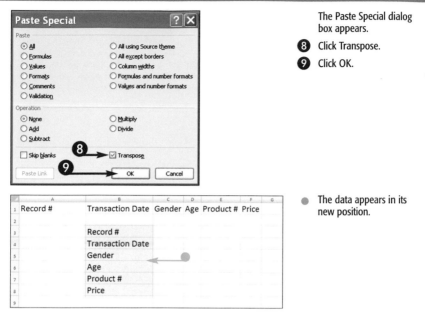

The Paste Special dialog box appears.

8 Click Transpose.

9 Click OK.

● The data appears in its new position.

TIP

Did You Know?

With the TRANSPOSE function, you can transpose a grid of cells. Start by selecting an area large enough to hold the new grid. In the Formula bar, type **=TRANSPOSE(** and then click the Insert Function icon. The Function Arguments dialog box appears. Click and drag to select the cells you want to transpose, and then press Ctrl+Shift+Enter. Excel transposes the grid.

With Office 2007, you can place content into a storage area called the Clipboard and paste the content into Excel or another Office application. The Office Clipboard can store up to 24 cut or copied items. All the items on the Clipboard are available for you to paste to a new location in Excel or in another Office document.

The Clipboard is not visible until you access it. In Excel, you can access the Clipboard by clicking the launcher in the Clipboard group of the Home tab. You can use the Clipboard to store a range of cells. The Office Clipboard pastes the entire range and includes all the values, but any formulas in the cells are not included.

① Click and drag to select the cells you want to copy.

② Click the Home tab.

③ Click the Copy icon.

Excel places a copy of the information on the Office Clipboard.

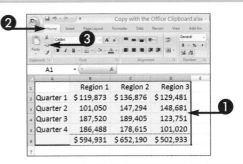

④ Click the Clipboard group launcher.

The Clipboard task pane appears.

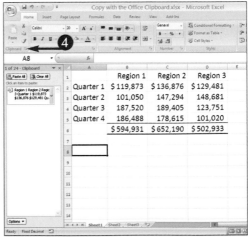

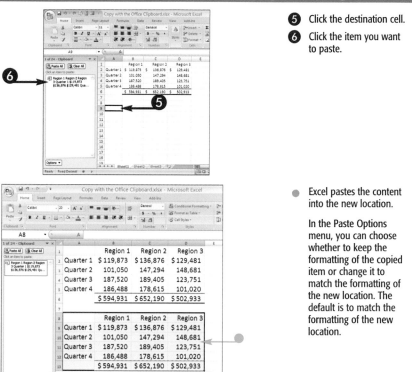

⑤ Click the destination cell.

⑥ Click the item you want to paste.

● Excel pastes the content into the new location.

In the Paste Options menu, you can choose whether to keep the formatting of the copied item or change it to match the formatting of the new location. The default is to match the formatting of the new location.

TIP

Did You Know?
The Office Clipboard holds graphical objects; so, you can use it to bring digital pictures, WordArt, and clip art from other programs into Excel.

Specify How to Paste with Paste Special

Cells can contain a lot of information. When you paste with Paste Special, you decide exactly what information you want to paste. You can choose to paste everything, or you can choose to paste just one element of the cell's contents, such as the formula, value, format, comment, validation, or column width.

You can Paste more than once. For example, when you paste by clicking the Paste icon, Excel pastes the values, formulas, and formats, but does not adjust the column widths. You can remedy this by pasting in two steps. In the first step, paste column widths, and Excel adjusts the column widths. In the second step, paste your values, formulas, and formats.

① Click and drag to select the cells you want to copy.

② Click the Home tab.

③ Click the Copy icon.

④ Place the cursor in the cell or cells in which you want to paste.

⑤ Click Paste.

   A menu appears.

⑥ Click Paste Special.

   The Paste Special dialog box appears.

⑦ Click Column widths.

⑧ Click OK.

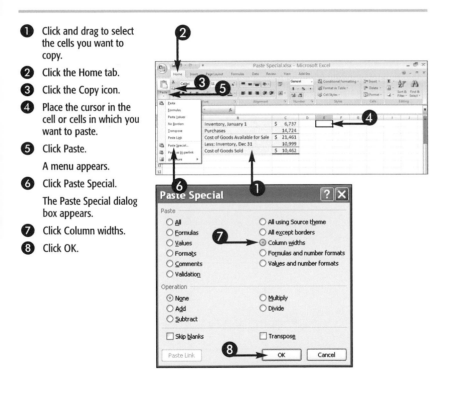

Excel copies the column widths from the source to the destination.

⑨ Click the Paste icon.

Excel copies the contents of the cells.

Press Esc to end the copy session.

TIP

Did You Know?

You can press Ctrl+C to copy. You can press Ctrl+V to paste. You can press Ctrl+X to cut. Cutting and pasting removes data from its current location and places it in a new location.

continued

You can use Paste Special to copy formats from one cell to another. You simply copy a cell with the format you want, and then use Paste Special to paste the format into other cells.

You can use the same steps to copy formulas or values from one location in your worksheet to another. When you want to use a cell's formula in other cells in your worksheet, paste the formula. When you want the results of a formula but not the actual value, paste the value.

You can also use Paste Special to perform simple arithmetic operations on each cell in a range.

⑩ Click a cell with the formula, value, or format you want to copy.

This example copies a formula.

⑪ Repeat steps 2 to 5.

The Paste Special dialog box appears.

⑫ Click to select a Paste option.

⑬ Click OK.

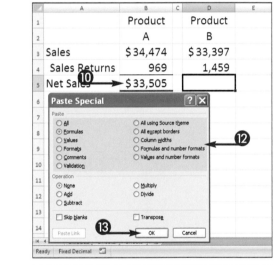

● Excel pastes.

If you paste a formula, an icon menu appears. You can click Formulas and Number Formatting to copy the number formatting as well as the formula.

	A	B	C	D	E	F
1	**ID**	**Products**	**Price**		1.1	⟵ ⑭
2	1	Combs	3.99			
3	2	Brushes	2.99			
4	3	Bands	5.99			
5	4	Hairspray	3.99			

Paste Special ？ ✕

Paste
- ⦿ A_ll
- ○ _F_ormulas
- ○ _V_alues
- ○ Forma_t_s
- ○ _C_omments
- ○ Validatio_n_

- ○ All using Source theme
- ○ All e_x_cept borders
- ○ Column _w_idths
- ○ Fo_r_mulas and number formats
- ○ Val_u_es and number formats

Operation
- ○ N_o_ne
- ○ A_d_d
- ○ _S_ubtract

- ⦿ _M_ultiply ⟵ ⑯
- ○ D_i_vide

☐ Skip _b_lanks   ☐ Transpos_e_

Paste Link ⑰ [OK] [Cancel]

Select destination and press ENTER or choose Paste   Averag

	A	B	C	D	E	F
1	**ID**	**Products**	**Price**		1.1	
2	1	Combs	4.389			
3	2	Brushes	3.289	⟵ ●		
4	3	Bands	6.589			
5	4	Hairspray	4.389			
6						
7						

⑭ Click a cell with the number by which you want to add, subtract, multiply, or divide.

⑮ Repeat steps 2 to 5.

The Paste Special dialog box appears.

⑯ Click an operation.

⑰ Click OK.

Excel performs the operation you selected.

● In this example, Excel multiplies each price by 1.10.

TIP

Did You Know?
You can use the Paste Link option in the Paste Special dialog box to keep your source and destination data synchronized. If you click the Paste Link button, when you make changes to the source data, Excel automatically updates the destination data. However, the reverse is not true; if you change your destination data, Excel does not update your source data.

By using Excel's many format options, you can easily format numbers, text, and cells. A style is a named collection of formats. Styles streamline the work of formatting so that you and others can apply a consistent set of formats to worksheet elements, such as row heads, column heads, and data values. Excel comes with many styles, and you can create your own.

To create a new style based on a current one, right-click the style and then click Modify. In the Style dialog box that appears, click Format. The Cells dialog box appears, where you can select one or more formats. Click OK when you are finished. Back in the Style dialog box, give your new style a name, and then click OK.

GROUP FORMATS AS A STYLE

① Click a cell with formats you want to use as the basis for a style.

② Click the Home tab.

③ Click Cell Style.

The Styles gallery appears.

④ Click New Cell Style.

The Style dialog box appears.

⑤ Type a name for your style.

⑥ Click OK.

You can now apply the style throughout the current workbook.

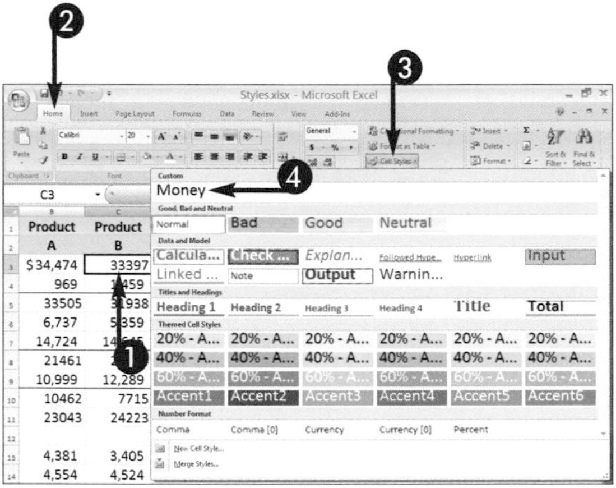

APPLY A FORMAT STYLE

① Click and drag to select the cells to which you want to apply the style.

② Click the Home tab.

③ Click Cell Styles.

The Styles gallery appears.

④ Click the style you created.

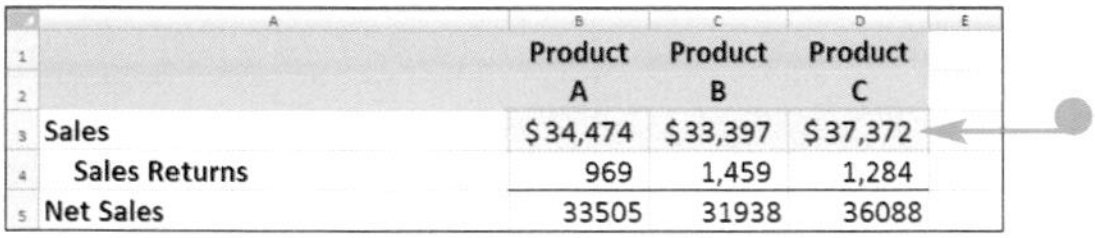

● Excel applies the style.

	A	B	C	D	E
1		Product A	Product B	Product C	
3	Sales	$34,474	$33,397	$37,372	
4	Sales Returns	969	1,459	1,284	
5	Net Sales	33505	31938	36088	

TIP

Apply It!
You can build a style from the ground up, rather than basing it on a formatted cell. Click a cell to receive the style, click the Home tab, and then click Cell Styles. The Styles gallery appears. Click New Cell Style, and then in the Style dialog box, click Format. The Format Cells dialog box appears. You can use it to design your style.

A style is a collection of formats you use within a workbook. With styles, you maintain consistency in the way numbers, dates, times, borders, and text appear in cells.

You can create a style based on any combination of formats available in the Format Cells dialog box, which you access by clicking the Format button in the Styles dialog box. One workbook can contain many styles.

Copying a style into another workbook is called merging. To merge styles, you need to open both the workbook from which you want to copy the style and the workbook to which you want to apply it.

① Open the file with your custom style.

② Open the workbook into which you want to merge styles.

③ Click the Home tab.

④ Click Cell Styles.

The Styles gallery appears.

⑤ Click Merge Styles.

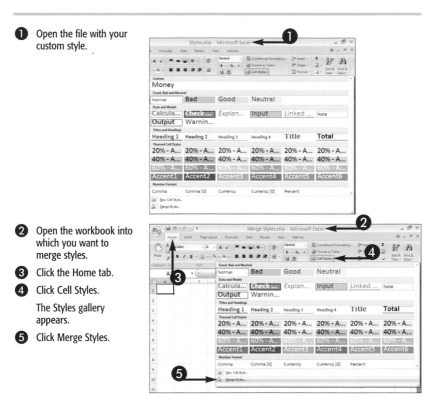

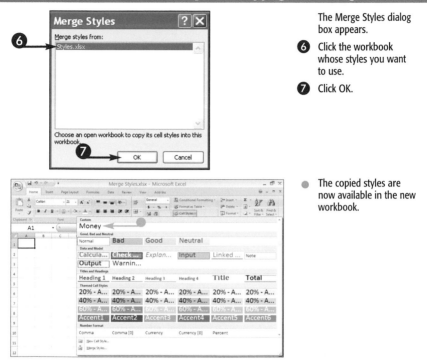

The Merge Styles dialog box appears.

6 Click the workbook whose styles you want to use.

7 Click OK.

● The copied styles are now available in the new workbook.

TIP

Did You Know?

Each style in a workbook must have a unique name. If you try to copy a style into a workbook that contains a style with the same name, a warning box appears when you click OK in the Merge Styles dialog box. If you want the imported style to take the place of the existing style, click OK. Otherwise, click No or Cancel.

Conditionally Format a Worksheet

If you want to monitor your data by highlighting certain conditions, Excel's conditional formatting feature can help you. For example, if your company offers a bonus whenever sales exceed $150,000, you can have Excel highlight cells containing sales figures whenever the value is more than $150,000.

You can also have Excel highlight a cell when the entry is less than, between, or equal to a specified value. You can use Excel's conditional formatting feature to monitor text, dates, duplicate values, the top N, the top N percent, the bottom N, the bottom N percent, above-average values, or below-average values.

CONDITIONAL FORMAT

① Click and drag to select the data you want to monitor.

② Click the Home tab.

③ Click Conditional Formatting.

A menu appears.

④ Click to select a menu option.

A submenu appears.

⑤ Click to select a menu option.

A dialog box appears.

This example uses Greater Than.

⑥ Type your criteria.

⑦ Click here and select the formatting you want to apply.

You can choose to create a custom format.

⑧ Click OK.

Excel highlights all of the data that meets your criteria.

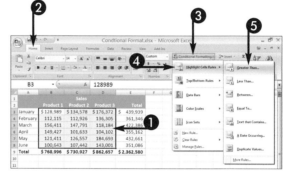

DATA BARS

① Repeat steps 1 to 3 under Conditional Format.

A menu appears.

② Click Data Bars.

A sub-menu appears

③ Click the color data bar you want to use.

	A	B	C	D	E	F
1			Sales			
2		Product 1	Product 2	Product 3	Total	
3	January	$ 128,989	$ 134,578	$ 176,372	$ 439,939	
4	February	112,115	112,926	136,305	361,346	
5	March	156,411	147,791	118,184	422,386	
6	April	149,427	101,633	104,102	355,162	
7	May	121,411	126,557	184,693	432,661	
8	June	100,643	107,442	143,001	351,086	
9	Total	$ 768,996	$ 730,927	$ 862,657	$ 2,362,580	
10						
11						

● Excel applies the data bars to the cells you selected.

Did You Know?

Excel provides you with several colors to choose from when adding data bars and color scales to your worksheet. You can select another color by clicking More Rules on both the Data Bars or Color Scales menu and then selecting the color you want in the New Formatting Rule dialog box.

continued

65

Data bars enable you to discern at a glance how large a value in one cell is relative to the values in other cells. A data bar is a colored bar you place in a cell. The length of the bar represents the value of the cell relative to other cells — the longer the bar, the higher the value.

Color scales and icon sets are similar to data bars, except color scales use gradients of color to represent cell value, and icon sets use icons to represent cell value.

Data bars, color scales, and icon sets all use rules to determine when to display what. You can use the rules defined by Excel, or you can create your own rule.

MODIFY RULES

① Repeat steps 1 to 3 under Conditional Format.

● This is selected data.

A menu appears.

② Click Icon Sets.

Alternatively, you can click Data Bars or Color Scales. Each selection allows you to change the associated rules.

③ Click More Rules.

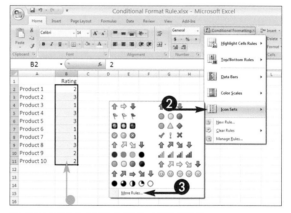

The New Formatting Rule dialog box appears.

④ Click here and select a format style.

⑤ Click here and select an operator.

⑥ Type a value or click the cell that contains the value you want to use.

⑦ Click here and select a type.

You can choose from Number, Percent, Formula, and Percentile.

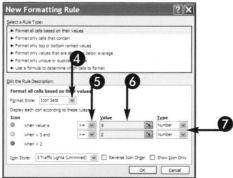

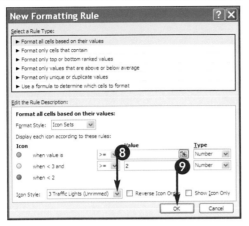

⑧ Click here and select an icon style.

⑨ Click OK.

Excel displays the results of your rule.

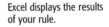

	A	B	C
1		Rating	
2	Product 1	○ 2	
3	Product 2	○ 3	
4	Product 3	● 1	
5	Product 4	○ 3	
6	Product 5	○ 3	
7	Product 6	● 1	
8	Product 7	● 1	
9	Product 8	○ 3	
10	Product 9	○ 2	
11	Product 10	○ 2	
12			
13			

TIP

Did You Know?

If you click the Show Icon Only, Show Bar Only, or Show Color Only option in the New Formatting Rule dialog box, depending on the option you select, Excel displays the icons, bars, or colors, but not the values in each cell.

Track Changes While Editing

If several people work on the same worksheet in a networked environment, you may need to account for who makes what changes, in which cells, and when. To do so, you can use the Track Changes feature.

In the Highlight Changes dialog box, use the When, Who, and Where options. Use When to define the time after which edits

are tracked — for example, after a specific date, or since you last saved the worksheet. Use Who to identify the group whose edits you want to track — for example, everyone in the workgroup, everyone but you, or a named individual. Use Where to specify the rows and columns whose data you want to monitor.

① Click the Review tab.
② Click Track Changes.
   A menu appears.
③ Click Highlight Changes.

   The Highlight Changes dialog box appears.
④ Click to select the Track changes while editing option.

   The optional When, Who, and Where fields become available.

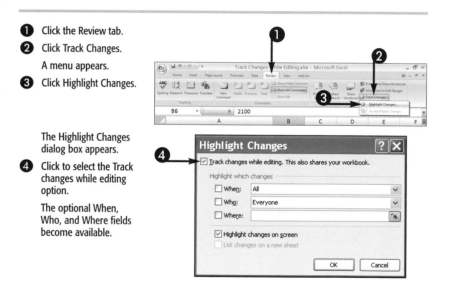

Highlight Changes

☑ Track changes while editing. This also shares your workbook.

Highlight which changes

☑ When: Since I last saved

☑ Who: Everyone

☑ Where: $B$6:$G$9

☑ Highlight changes on screen

☐ List changes on a new sheet

OK   Cancel

⑤ Click here and select when to track changes.

⑥ Click here and select whose changes to track.

⑦ Type the cell range, or click and drag to select the cells you want to monitor.

⑧ Click Highlight changes on screen to insert a purple flag into edited cells.

⑨ Click OK.

A message informs you that Excel has saved the workbook.

4		Jul-07	Aug-07	Sep-07	Oct-07	Nov
5	**Cash Receipts**					
6	Painting Interior	$ 2,200	$ 2,300	Denise Etheridge, 9/28/2006 9:40 PM:		
7	Painting Exterior	8,000	8,000	Changed cell C6 from '$2,000.00' to '$2,300.00'		
8	Drywall	1,500	1,500			
9	Roofing	3,000	3,000	3,000	,000	1,5
10	**Total Cash Receipts**	$14,700	$14,800	$14,000	$14,100	$11,5

● Purple flags appear in edited cells.

● To view a cell's comment, move your cursor over the cell.

Note: For more about comments, see Chapter 1.

TIP

Did You Know?
You can review every change made to a worksheet and either accept or reject the change. Click the Review tab, click Track Changes, and then click Accept/Reject Changes. The available options let you restrict your review to changes by certain people or at certain times.

Consolidate Worksheets

If you keep related data in separate worksheets, or for that matter separate workbooks, you may eventually want to consolidate your data. For example, if you keep sales information for several regions on separate worksheets, you may want to consolidate the worksheets to find the total sales for all regions. Excel's Consolidate feature allows you to do just that. Excel provides a variety of functions you can use

to consolidate, including Sum, Count, Average, Max, Min, and Product.

You start the consolidation process by selecting the location for your consolidated data. You then select the function you want to use to consolidate. You tell Excel the location of the data you want to consolidate. Excel then takes the data and consolidates it.

① Click the top-left cell of the range into which you want to consolidate your data.

② Click the Data tab.

③ Click the Consolidate icon.

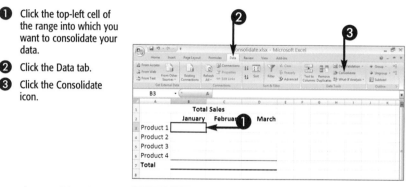

The Consolidate dialog box appears.

④ Click here and select the function you want to use to consolidate your data.

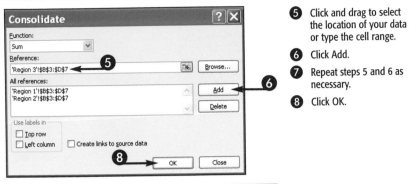

⑤ Click and drag to select the location of your data or type the cell range.

⑥ Click Add.

⑦ Repeat steps 5 and 6 as necessary.

⑧ Click OK.

Excel consolidates your data.

Consolidate

Function:
Sum

Reference:
'Region 3'!$B$3:$D$7 ⑤

All references:
'Region 1'!$B$3:$D$7
'Region 2'!$B$3:$D$7

Browse...

Add ⑥

Delete

Use labels in
☐ Top row
☐ Left column   ☐ Create links to source data

⑧ OK   Close

	Total Sales			
	January	February	March	
Product 1	$ 364,414	$ 416,103	$ 393,622	
Product 2	307,192	447,774	451,990	
Product 3	570,061	575,791	376,203	
Product 4	566,924	542,990	307,101	
Total	$ 1,784,793	$ 1,956,570	$ 1,508,799	

TIP

Did You Know?
You can include data from another workbook in your worksheet. Click the Browse button in the Consolidate dialog box. The Browse dialog box appears. You can use the Browse dialog box to locate the workbook you want to use in your consolidation. Click the filename and then click OK to open the file. Click and drag to specify the data you want to consolidate.

Manipulating Records

A table is a set of columns and rows. Each column represents a single type of data. For example, a table might have three columns representing name, gender, and age. Each row in the table is a record. For each record in the table, the name column contains a name, the gender column a gender, and the age column an age. When you structure a worksheet as a table, you can use Excel's database-like capabilities to go beyond what is possible with a simple worksheet.

This chapter shows you how to work with data that you have structured as a table. Much of the chapter focuses on sorting and filtering. To sort means to arrange a list in order, either alphabetically or numerically. You can sort and re-sort lists as necessary,

and even sort within a sort. To filter means to display only the information that meets certain criteria, while temporarily hiding the rest.

With data formatted as a table, you can count, average, and subtotal parts of your data that meet certain criteria. For example, in a customer survey, you can count the number of senior citizens who prefer a certain sport.

When you organize data into a table, you have access to lookups, which are a special way of searching for data. For example, you might use a lookup to retrieve a stock price by typing in a stock symbol. You can also create a powerful analytical tool called a PivotTable, discussed in Chapter 5.

Enter Data with a Form 74

Filter Duplicate Records..76

Perform Simple Sorts and Filters 78

Perform Complex Sorts 80

Perform Complex Filters 82

Filter by Multiple Criteria in the Same Column.........................84

Subtotal Sorted Data 86

Chart Filtered Data Easily 88

Count Filtered Records 90

Look Up Information in a Worksheet 92

Define Data as a Table...94

Modify a Table Style..96

Excel enables you to generate a form to simplify data entry. A form simplifies and speeds up data entry by providing a blank field for each column in your table. You can type in the fields and use the Tab key to move from field to field. You can move backward and forward through your list

to view or modify your data. The table form doubles as a search box you can use to retrieve values in a worksheet.

You must add the Form icon to the Quick Access toolbar before you can use forms. See Chapter 10 to learn how to add an icon to the Quick Access toolbar.

① Type your column heads.

② Click and drag to select the column heads.

③ Click the Form icon.

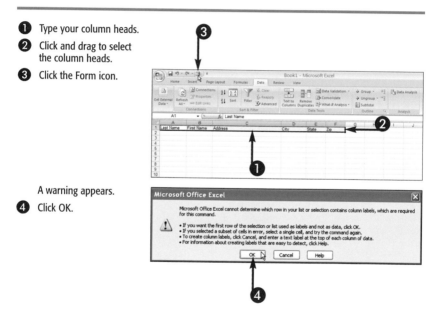

A warning appears.

④ Click OK.

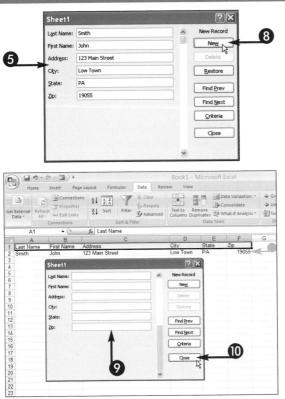

The data form appears, consisting of one field for each column head you created.

⑤ Type the requested information in each field.

⑥ Press Tab to move to the next field.

⑦ Repeat steps 5 and 6 to complete the remaining fields.

⑧ After completing a first set of fields, click New to start a new record.

● The data fills the worksheet, and the form fields clear, ready for another record.

⑨ Repeat steps 5 to 8 for each new record.

⑩ Click Close after entering your data.

A list of your data records appears in the worksheet.

TIP

Did You Know?

After you enter data, you can use the data form to search for and edit your data. With the list and form displayed, click the form's Criteria button. In a blank field, type an operator, such as = or >, and a value in one or more fields. For example, to find all records for Sally, you would type **=Sally** in the Name field and press Enter. If several records are available, click the Find Prev (Previous) and Find Next buttons as appropriate.

Filter Duplicate Records

Excel provides many tools for managing long tables. With these tables, you may find that you need to identify and display unique records. For example, a baseball-card collector, may want to find the number of unique players represented in his collection so that he can create a catalog.

Excel provides tools for displaying only unique records in a table. You start with a worksheet formatted as a table in which some of the records are duplicates. You can then use Excel's advanced filtering tools to identify and remove from view the duplicated records.

If you want to remove duplicate records permanently, use the Remove Duplicates feature on the Data tab.

---

① Click a cell in your list.

② Click the Data tab.

③ Click Advanced.

The Advanced Filter dialog box appears.

④ Click to select the Filter the list, in–place option.

⑤ Click and drag to select your entire list, or type the cell range.

⑥ Click to select the Unique records only option.

⑦ Click OK.

	A	B	C	D	E	F
1	**Last Name**	**First Name**	**Company**	**City**	**State**	
2	Mayfield	Adam	York, LLC	Boston	MA	
3	Johns	Sam	London Group	Philadelphia	PA	
4	Lorne	Harry	AVS	Philadelphia	PA	
5	Jacs	Henry	Labcaster, Corp	Chicago	IL	
6	Mathews	John	CMO Group	San Francisco	CA	
7	Jones	Libby	The James Company	Washington	DC	
8	Bradley	Florence	Fed Mexico	Philadelphia	PA	
9	Hilton	Mary	CVP	San Francisco	CA	
10	Wilks	Sally	Stein & Jacobs	Boston	MA	
15	Baldwin	Serena	Universal America	San Francisco	CA	
16	Hicks	Taylor	Labcaster, Corp	Chicago	IL	
18	Ling	Wei	The James Company	Washington	DC	
21						

Excel filters the duplicate records.

- You can tell the records are hidden because the row numbers are not continuous.

⑧ Click the Data tab.

⑨ Click Clear.

The duplicate records display.

TIP

Did You Know?

Filtering duplicate records temporarily removes them from view. If you want to delete duplicate records permanently, click the Data tab and then click Remove Duplicates. The Remove Duplicates dialog box appears. Select the columns you want to check for duplicates, and then click OK. Excel deletes the duplicate records.

Sorting and filtering your lists offers different ways to view your data. When you sort, you rearrange your data in ascending, A to Z, or descending, Z to A, order. When you arrange a list in a familiar order, you can easily find data, group data, and present it meaningfully to others.

Filtering works like a sieve through which you pass your data, and displays only data that meets your criteria. For example, in a customer survey, you can choose to view only customers who live in a certain state or city or who are of a certain age or gender.

SORT A LIST

1. Click a cell in a list.
2. Click the Data tab.
3. Click a sort direction.

   Click A to Z to sort from lowest to highest – ascending order.

   Click Z to A to sort from highest to lowest – descending order.

   Excel sorts your list.

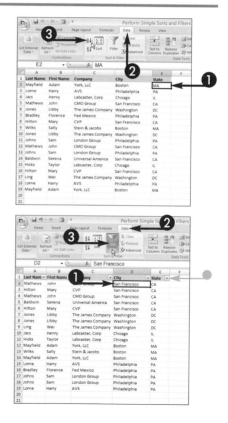

FILTER A LIST

1. Click a cell in the list.
2. Click the Data tab.
3. Click Filter.

● Down-arrows appear next to your field headers.

④

	A	B	C	D	E	F
1	Last Nam ▼	First Name ▼	Company ▼	City ▼	State ▼	
2	Mathews	John	CMC		CA	
3	Hilton	Mary	CVP	Sort A to Z	CA	
4	Mathews	John	CMC	Sort Z to A	CA	
5	Baldwin	Serena	Univ	Sort by Color ▶	CA	
6	Hilton	Mary	CVP	Clear Filter From "City"	CA	
7	Jones	Libby	The	Filter by Color ▶	DC	
8	Jones	Libby	The	Text Filters ▶	DC	
9	Ling	Wei	The		DC	
10	Jacs	Henry	Lab	☐ (Select All)	IL	
11	Hicks	Taylor	b	☑ Boston	IL	
12	Mayfield	Adam	ri	☑ Chicago	MA	
13	Wilks	Sally	Stei	☐ Philadelphia	MA	
14	Mayfield	Adam	York	☐ San Francisco	MA	
15	Lorne	Harry	AVS	☐ Washington	PA	
16	Bradley	Florence	Fed		PA	
17	Johns	Sam			PA	
18	Johns	Sam	L	OK Cancel	PA	
19	Lorne	Harry	AVS		PA	
20						

⑤

⑥

④ Click a down-arrow.

A drop-down menu appears.

⑤ Click to deselect the items that you do not want to appear.

⑥ Click OK.

	A	B	C	D	E	F
1	Last Nam ▼	First Name ▼	Company ▼	City ▼	State ▼	
10	Jacs	Henry	Labcaster, Corp	Chicago	IL	
11	Hicks	Taylor	Labcaster, Corp	Chicago	IL	
12	Mayfield	Adam	York, LLC	Boston	MA	
13	Wilks	Sally	Stein & Jacobs	Boston	MA	
14	Mayfield	Adam	York, LLC	Boston	MA	
20						
21						

Excel filters the list.

Did You Know?

Your data is either continuous or discrete. Continuous data assumes a wide variety of values, such as incomes and names. Discrete data assumes only a few values, such as male or female. Sorting continuous data imposes order by alphabetizing it or ranking it numerically. Sorting discrete data has the effect of grouping similar values so that you can compare one category with another.

Perform Complex Sorts

Sorting a list by one criterion, such as age, arranges your records for easy scanning. You can also sort by multiple criteria — a sort within a sort. For example, after sorting your customer records by community, you can sort them by gender.

You define sorts in the Sort dialog box. Keep in mind that ascending and descending are not your only sort choices; you can click the Options button to specify a custom order. For example, you could order months chronologically from January to December, instead of alphabetically from April to November.

---

① Click a cell in your list.

② Click the Data tab.

③ Click Sort.

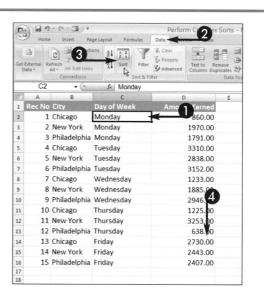

The Sort dialog box appears.

④ Click here and select the column by which you want to sort.

⑤ Click here and select values on which you want to sort.

⑥ Click here and select a sort order.

⑦ Click Add Level.

⑧ Repeat steps 5 to 7 to sort by additional criteria.

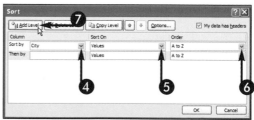

9 Click here and select Custom List.

The Custom Lists dialog box appears.

10 Click to sort by days of the week or months of the year.

11 Click OK.

12 Click OK.

The list sorts according to the sort order that you specified, along with any options that you chose.

	A	B	C	D	E
1	Rec No	City	Day of Week	Amount Earned	
2	1	Chicago	Monday	860.00	
3	4	Chicago	Tuesday	3310.00	
4	7	Chicago	Wednesday	1233.00	
5	10	Chicago	Thursday	1225.00	
6	13	Chicago	Friday	2730.00	
7	2	New York	Monday	1970.00	
8	5	New York	Tuesday	2838.00	
9	8	New York	Wednesday	1885.00	
10	11	New York	Thursday	3253.00	
11	14	New York	Friday	2443.00	
12	3	Philadelphia	Monday	1791.00	
13	6	Philadelphia	Tuesday	3152.00	
14	9	Philadelphia	Wednesday	2946.00	
15	12	Philadelphia	Thursday	638.00	
16	15	Philadelphia	Friday	2407.00	
17					
18					

TIP

Did You Know?
You can delete and copy sort levels. In the Sort dialog box, click Delete Level to delete a sort level. Click Copy Level to copy a sort level. Click ⊞ to move a sort level up, and click ⊞ to move a sort level down.

Perform Complex Filters

Whereas sorting rearranges all records in ascending or descending order, filtering enables you to see only the records that match your criteria, while hiding the rest. Criteria can look like this: `Age > 65` and `State = "Missouri"`, where Age and State are the names of column heads. When you filter a list, down-arrows appear to the right of every column head.

Click a column's down-arrow to select values by which you want to filter the column. By applying a filter, you display only those records that contain certain values in the column, such as all men who live in a specific community. By applying several filters, you can quickly narrow down a long list to the few records that interest you.

---

1 Click a cell in your list.

2 Click the Data tab.

3 Click Filter.

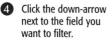

Down-arrows appear next to all of your column heads.

4 Click the down-arrow next to the field you want to filter.

5 Click Number Filters if you choose a number field.

Alternatively, you can click Text Filters if you choose a text field.

6 Click Custom Filter.

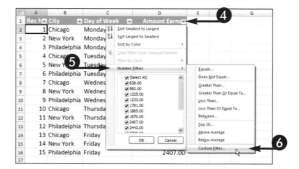

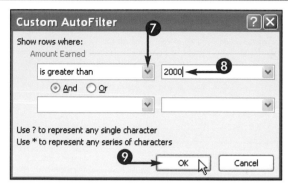

The Custom AutoFilter dialog box appears.

7 Click here and select an operator.

8 Type a value or select a value.

You can repeat steps 7 and 8 if you want to create a second criterion. Choose And if you want both criteria to be met. Choose Or if you want either criterion to be met.

9 Click OK.

The list displays records matching your criteria.

To sort the filtered records, you can click the Data tab, and then click a sort option.

	A	B	C	D	E
1	Rec N	City	Day of Week	Amount Earned	
5	4	Chicago	Tuesday	3310.00	
6	5	New York	Tuesday	2838.00	
7	6	Philadelphia	Tuesday	3152.00	
10	9	Philadelphia	Wednesday	2946.00	
12	11	New York	Thursday	3253.00	
14	13	Chicago	Friday	2730.00	
15	14	New York	Friday	2443.00	
16	15	Philadelphia	Friday	2407.00	
17					
18					

TIP

Did You Know?
In the Filtering menu, click Sort Ascending or Sort Descending to sort the filtered records. Click Top 10 to view the top ten values, or click Bottom 10 for the bottom ten values. You can also choose a number other than ten. To apply more than one filter to a column — for example, Age < 20 or Age > 30 — click Custom Filter.

Filter by Multiple Criteria in the Same Column

With advanced filtering, you can create more than two filters for a single column. For example, you can filter a survey to find people of age 30 or younger who earn more than $35,000, and people of age 35 or older who earn more than $45,000.

Advanced filtering requires a bit of work, even when you are using the Advanced Filter menu command. You must find a block of cells on the worksheet and create a criteria range. When creating a criteria range, use one or more column heads from a list. In the cell below each head, type criteria by which to filter each column, such as <30 and >35000.

---

① On the worksheet with your list, type the column head names of the columns that you want to filter.

② Type criteria by which to filter values.

You must use operators to define criteria, and place text in quotes.

	A	B	C	D	E	F	G	H	I
1	Rec-No	ID Number	Gender	Age	Income		Age	Income	
2	1	60-589	M	28	78,298		<30	>35000	
3	2	75-848	M	56	30,962		>35	>40000	
4	3	14-225	F	62	124,310				
5	4	19-762	F	63	46,866				
6	5	54-278	M	26	125,079				
7	6	94-848	F	46	68,510				
8	7	77-909	M	23	29,940				
9	8	28-016	F	61	115,827				
10	9	31-423	M	23	117,466				
11	10	66-833	M	55	99,951				
12	11	44-548	M	22	33,514				
13	12	54-978	M	33	94,559				
14	13	57-911	F	22	58,581				
15	14	92-800	F	32	79,857				
16	15	93-258	M	57	123,925				
17	16	87-115	M	44	63,815				
18	17	53-088	F	22	63,390				
19	18	38-389	F	47	43,971				
20	19	19-035	F	35	60,242				
21	20	29-424	M	44	29,749				
22	21	75-453	M	55	126,703				

Ready   Sheet1   Sheet2   Sheet3

③ Click the Data tab.

④ Click Advanced.

Filter by Multiple Criteria - Microsoft Excel

Home   Insert   Page Layout   Formulas   Data

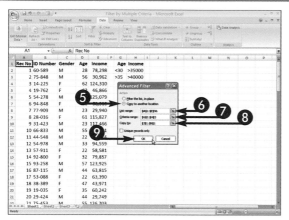

The Advanced Filter dialog box appears.

⑤ Click to indicate where to place the filtered list.

⑥ Type the range for the entire list.

⑦ Type the range for the criteria defined in step 2.

⑧ If you chose to copy the filtered list in step 5, click the first cell for the filter.

⑨ Click OK.

The filtered list appears.

You may need to format the results to accommodate wide columns.

Caution!

Make sure that your "Copy to" range has enough room below it to include all of the values that may return in the filtered list. If you place the "Copy to" range above your original list, the results may overwrite the list and disrupt the filtering. Placing the copy to the side of the list or below it protects your original list.

Subtotal Sorted Data

After you sort and group your data into categories such as gender or age, you can perform a calculation on each category. Excel provides the tools for performing simple calculations to compare one category with another.

With a sort defined for at least one column, you can find the average, sum, minimum, maximum, number of items, and much more for that column or another column. Excel calls the feature that enables you to perform calculations on columns subtotaling, even though you can use it to do more than subtotal. Subtotaling also uses outlining to hide data so that you can compare rows or columns.

---

① Click a cell in your sorted list.

② Click the Data tab.

③ Click Subtotal.

The Subtotal dialog box appears.

④ Click here and select the category by which you want to subtotal.

⑤ Click here and select the type of calculation.

⑥ Click one or more columns to subtotal.

⑦ Click OK.

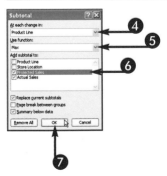

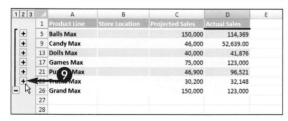

1 2 3		A	B	C	D	E
	1	Product Line	Store Location	Projected Sales	Actual Sales	
	2	Balls	NJ	15,000	14,279	
	3	Balls	DE	2,400	14,279	
	4	Balls	PA	150,000	114,369	
	5	Balls Max		150,000	114,369	
	6	Candy	NJ	23,000	21,569	
	7	Candy	DE	8,000	7,654	
	8	Candy	PA	46,000	52,639.00	
	9	Candy Max		46,000	52,639.00	
	10	Dolls	NJ	20,000	19,562.00	
	11	Dolls	DE	2,000	19,562	
	12	Dolls	PA	40,000	41,876	
	13	Dolls Max		40,000	41,876	
	14	Games	NJ	75,000	123,000	
	15	Games	DE	4,500	123,000	
	16	Games	PA	8,000	7,812	
	17	Games Max		75,000	123,000	
	18	Puzzles	NJ	5,000	2,187	
	19	Puzzles	DE	1,000	2,187	
	20	Puzzles	PA	46,900	96,521	
	21	Puzzles Max		46,900	96,521	
	22	Trucks	NJ	30,200	31,248	
	23	Trucks	DE	15,200	31,248	
	24	Trucks	PA	30,000	32,148	
	25	Trucks Max		30,200	32,148	
	26	Grand Max		150,000	123,000	
	27					

The list appears with the outlining controls that enable you to compare the results.

⑧ To compare results in different rows, click the minus sign.

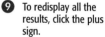

1 2 3		A	B	C	D	E
	1	Product Line	Store Location	Projected Sales	Actual Sales	
	5	Balls Max		150,000	114,369	
	9	Candy Max		46,000	52,639.00	
	13	Dolls Max		40,000	41,876	
	17	Games Max		75,000	123,000	
	21	Puzzles Max		46,900	96,521	
	25	Trucks Max		30,200	32,148	
	26	Grand Max		150,000	123,000	
	27					
	28					

Only the result rows appear.

⑨ To redisplay all the results, click the plus sign.

TIP

Did You Know?

You can create several subtotals for a single sorted list. To display all of your subtotals, make sure the Replace current subtotals check box is not checked when you use the Subtotal dialog box. You can remove outlining by clicking the Data tab, Outline, Ungroup, and then Clear Outline.

With Excel, you can quickly create a chart showing the information in a worksheet or list. Charts show trends and anomalies that may otherwise be difficult to detect in columns of numbers. For more about charts, see Chapter 6.

You can position your chart next to the data on which you based it, so when you change the data, you can instantly observe the changes in the chart. By default, as you filter your data, Excel removes the filtered data from your chart. If you do not want Excel to remove the filtered data from your chart, select the Show data in hidden rows and columns option in the Hidden and Empty Cell Settings dialog box.

① **Create a chart.**

Note: *See Chapter 6 for detailed information on creating charts.*

② **Filter the data on which the chart is based.**

● A filter icon on the down-arrow icon indicates that you have filtered data.

By default, only the filtered data displays in the chart.

③ **Click your chart.**

● The Chart Tools become available.

④ **Click the Design tab.**

⑤ **Click Select Data.**

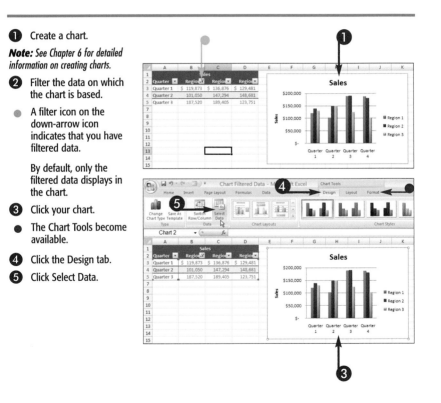

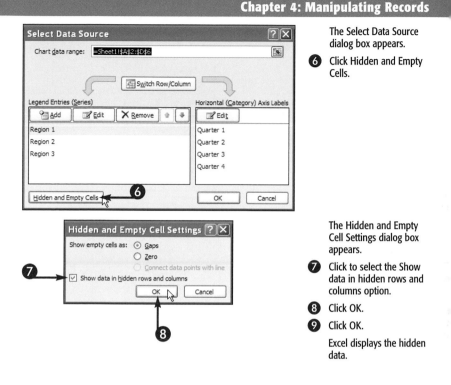

The Select Data Source dialog box appears.

⑥ Click Hidden and Empty Cells.

The Hidden and Empty Cell Settings dialog box appears.

⑦ Click to select the Show data in hidden rows and columns option.

⑧ Click OK.

⑨ Click OK.

Excel displays the hidden data.

TIP

Did You Know?
If you want to reposition a chart, click the chart. A border with triple dots appears on all four sides of the chart and on the corners. Roll your cursor over the dots. When it turns into a four-headed arrow, you can click and drag your chart.

Count Filtered Records

Like the standard worksheet functions, database functions enable you to perform calculations and summarize data. Database functions are especially good at summarizing the subsets you created from your list by filtering. Most database functions combine two tasks: They filter a group of records based on values in a single column, and then they count them or perform another simple operation on the filtered data.

DCOUNT is a database function that counts the number of cells containing a number. DCOUNT takes three arguments. The first argument, **Database**, identifies the cell range for the entire list. The second argument, **Field**, identifies the cell range for the column from which you want to extract data. In the third argument, **Criteria**, you provide Excel a criterion for extracting information.

① Insert several rows above your list to hold the criteria range.

② Type the column head for which you want to count records.

③ Type the criterion for counting records.

④ Click a cell to hold your formula.

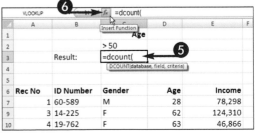

⑤ Type **=DCOUNT(**.

Alternatively, click the function on the auto-complete list.

⑥ Click the Insert Function icon.

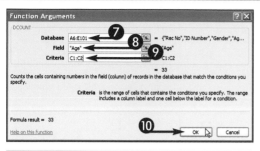

	A	B	C	D	E	F
1			**Age**			
2			> 50			
3		Result:	33			
4						
5						
6	**Rec No**	**ID Number**	**Gender**	**Age**	**Income**	
7	1	60-589	M	28	78,298	
9	3	14-225	F	62	124,310	
10	4	19-762	F	63	46,866	
11	5	54-278	M	26	125,079	
12	6	94-848	F	46	68,510	
14	8	28-016	F	61	115,827	
15	9	31-423	M	23	117,466	
16	10	66-833	M	55	99,951	
19	13	57-911	F	22	58,581	
21	15	93-258	M	57	123,925	
22	16	87-115	M	44	63,815	
23	17	53-088	F	22	63,390	
24	18	38-389	F	47	43,971	
27	21	75-453	M	55	126,703	
28	22	64-889	F	42	84,736	
29	23	40-263	F	61	144,108	

The Function Arguments dialog box appears.

⑦ Click and drag all the cells in the list, or type the cell range.

⑧ Type the column name within quotation marks.

You can also type the column's number or the column's range.

⑨ Click and drag the cell range that you specified in steps 2 and 3.

⑩ Click OK.

● The result appears.

The DCOUNT *function counts only cells containing numbers. For non-numeric data, you can use the* DCOUNTA *function.*

Did You Know?

You can use the DSUM function to add numbers that match the criteria you specify. You can use DAVERAGE to find the average of numbers that match the criteria you specify. These functions use the same arguments as DCOUNT: database, field, and criteria range.

Look Up Information in a Worksheet

You can use the VLOOKUP function when you know one value and need to look up another value. Before you can use VLOOKUP, you must sort your list in ascending order, and the first column of your list must contain the values you want to use to retrieve another value. You specify the column from which you want to retrieve the corresponding value.

You can use the Function Wizard to enter your VLOOKUP arguments. You must enter three required arguments: the cell address containing the value you want to use to retrieve another value, the list's cell range, and the column that contains the value you want to retrieve. For simplicity, you can call the first column in the list 1, the second column 2, and so on.

---

① Type the value you want to use to retrieve another value.

② In an adjacent cell, type **=VLOOKUP(**.

As you begin to type, the function auto-complete list appears. You can click the function.

③ Click the Insert Function icon.

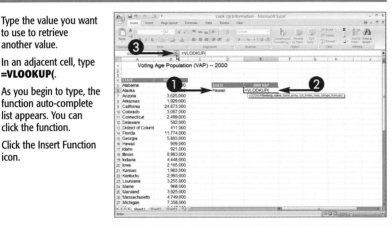

The Function Arguments dialog box appears.

④ Click the cell with the value you entered in step 1.

⑤ Click and drag to select all the values in the list, or type a cell range.

⑥ Type the number of the column containing the value you want to retrieve.

⑦ Click OK.

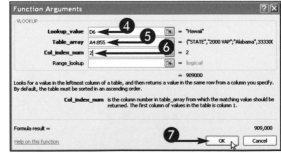

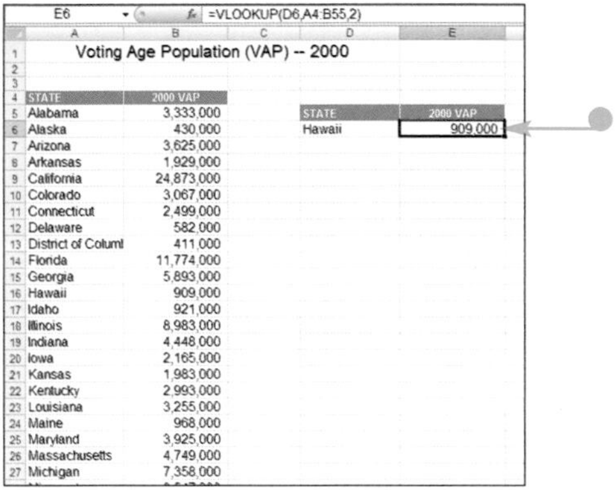

| E6 | | fx | =VLOOKUP(D6,A4:B55,2) |

Voting Age Population (VAP) -- 2000

- The box containing the formula displays the value corresponding to the lookup value.

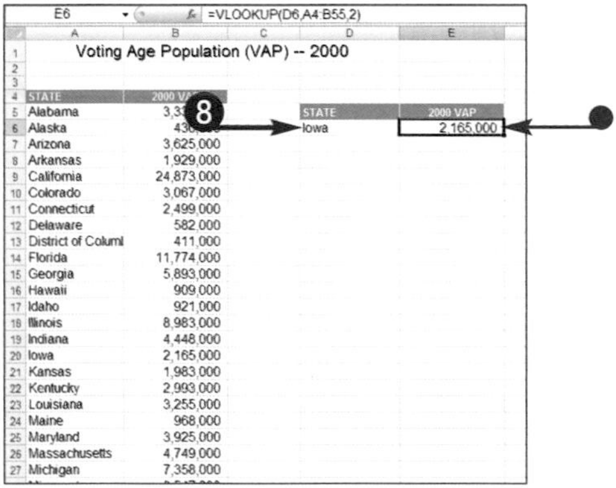

| E6 | | fx | =VLOOKUP(D6,A4:B55,2) |

Voting Age Population (VAP) -- 2000

⑧ Type another lookup value.

- The box containing the formula displays the value corresponding to the new lookup value.

TIP

Did You Know?

To simplify a function, give your list a name such as Sales or Customers. Likewise, you can use column names instead of column numbers to designate a column in which you can find the result. To learn how to name a range, see Chapter 1.

Define Data as a Table

You can define worksheet rows and columns as a table. When you define rows and columns as a table, sort and filter drop-down lists are automatically added to each column head, enabling you to readily sort and filter your data.

Defining a table is simple. In fact, you can define an existing worksheet as a table. Before you start, however, you must arrange your data in columns and rows, each with a descriptive column head.

Defining rows and columns as a table causes Table Tools to become available. You can use these design tools to format your table quickly. You should avoid blank cells and blank spaces at the beginning of a table cell because they make sorting difficult.

---

① Click and drag to select the data that you want to define as a table.

Include column heads.

② Click the Insert tab.

③ Click Table.

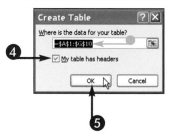

The Create Table dialog box appears.

● The data range you selected appears here.

④ Click to select this option if your table has headers.

⑤ Click OK.

Excel converts your data to a table.

● The Table Tools become available.

● Each column has a drop-down arrow. Click the arrow to sort and filter.

Note: *You can refer to the other sections of this chapter to learn how to sort and filter.*

⑥ Click the Design tab.

⑦ Click Total Row.

Excel places a total at the end of your table.

⑧ Click a field in the Total row.

A down-arrow appears next to the field.

⑨ Click the down-arrow and select how you want to total the column.

Excel totals your column.

Did You Know?

You can convert a table back to a regular range of cells. Click anywhere in your table, click the Design tab, and then click Convert to Range. When the prompt appears, click Yes. Excel converts the table to a normal range and removes the down-arrows.

Modify a
Table Style

Table styles format the rows and columns of your table to make the table easier to read. When you create a table, Excel applies the default style. You can easily change or remove any style that is applied to your table. Excel provides you with a large gallery of styles from which to choose.

Excel also provides a number of table-style options you can use to modify your table.

For example, by choosing banded rows or banded columns, you can have every other row or every other column appear in a different color. You can also apply special formatting to the last column or the first column in your table if you want the titles, totals, or information in those columns to stand out.

---

① Click any cell in your table.

The Table Tools become available.

② Click Table Styles.

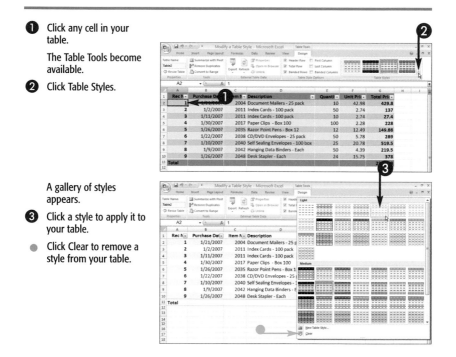

A gallery of styles appears.

③ Click a style to apply it to your table.

● Click Clear to remove a style from your table.

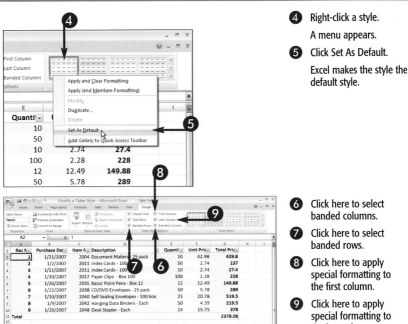

④ Right-click a style.

A menu appears.

⑤ Click Set As Default.

Excel makes the style the default style.

⑥ Click here to select banded columns.

⑦ Click here to select banded rows.

⑧ Click here to apply special formatting to the first column.

⑨ Click here to apply special formatting to the last column.

Excel formats your table.

TIP

Did You Know?

You can easily add columns to your table. When you click any cell in the table, the Table Tools become available. Click the Design tab and then click Resize Table. The Resize Table dialog box appears. Click and drag to select the new range, or type the range in the Select the new data range for your table field. Click OK.

Explore Patterns in Data

Excel offers you much more than a way of keeping track of your data and doing calculations. It also provides tools to analyze your data and thus to understand it better and to make better decisions. In this chapter, you find a range of tools that can give you many insights into your data.

One of the most useful tools, the PivotTable, is also one of the least understood. Similar to cross-tabulation in statistics, a PivotTable shows how data is distributed across categories. For example, you can analyze data and display how different products sell by region and by quarter. Alternatively, you can analyze income distribution and consumer preferences by gender and age bracket. Excel makes it easy for you to answer useful questions about your data.

This chapter also introduces Excel's statistical functions, with which you can analyze your data. These functions were once available only through large, expensive statistical software packages. You learn how to use descriptive statistics to characterize your data and to explore associations between data series by using the correlation function. For the statistically adept, Excel also includes more advanced functions.

In the final sections of the chapter, you learn how to do two related analytical tasks: what-if analysis and goal seeking. With what-if analysis, you vary an input to find how it affects a result. With goal seeking, you start with a goal and try to achieve it by varying a single factor.

Quick Tips

Create a PivotTable...100

Modify PivotTable Data and Layout..104

Compute Sub- and Grand Totals 106

Create a Calculated Field 108

Hide Columns or Rows in a PivotTable 110

Sort a PivotTable 111

Create a PivotChart...112

Describe Data with Statistics 114

Find the Correlation between Variables 116

Explore Outcomes with What-If Analysis 118

Optimize a Result with Goal Seek 120

Create a PivotTable

PivotTables help you answer questions about your data. The row and column labels of a PivotTable usually refer to discrete information, meaning the values fall into categories. For example, gender is a discrete variable, because all values are either male or female. Quarter is another discrete variable, because all values fall into one of four quarters — Quarter 1,

Quarter 2, Quarter 3, or Quarter 4. Salary and weight are not discrete but are continuous — a wide range of values is possible for each.

The body of a PivotTable — the data area — usually has continuous data to show how the data are distributed across rows and columns.

---

① Click and drag to select the data you want to include in your PivotTable.

You must include the row and column headings.

② Click the Insert tab.

③ Click PivotTable.

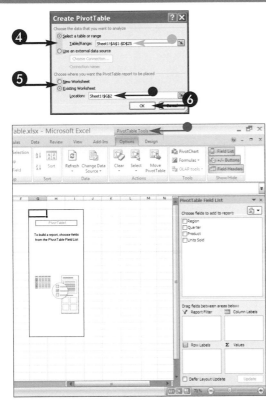

The Create PivotTable dialog box appears.

④ Click a data source.

● If you selected a range in the current workbook, the range appears here.

⑤ Click to select where to place the report.

● If you want to place the report in the existing worksheet, type a location.

⑥ Click OK.

Excel opens the PivotTable Field List.

● PivotTable Tools become available.

TIP

Caution!
You base PivotTables on lists. When creating a PivotTable, do not use a list with blank columns or rows, because Excel may not create the PivotTable correctly if the list includes a blank column or row.

The PivotTable layout consists of several elements: report filters, data, columns, and rows. You can use the PivotTable Field List to organize these elements. When working with a PivotTable, you can bring the Field List into view by clicking anywhere in the PivotTable, then clicking the Options tab, and then clicking Field List.

Report fields enable you to filter the data that appears in your report. Row fields appear as row labels down the left side of your PivotTable, and column fields appear as column labels across the top of your PivotTable. You place your continuous data fields in the Values box. Fields placed in the Values box make up the data area. You can also arrange and rearrange field layouts.

7 Click to select the fields you want to include in your PivotTable.

8 Click and drag fields among the Report, Column, Row Lab, and Values boxes.

● Fields you want to filter by.

● Fields you want to display as columns.

● Fields you want to display as rows.

● Fields you want to display as data.

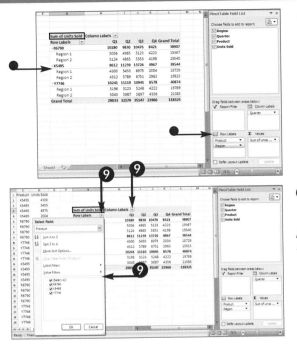

● As you build the PivotTable, your changes instantly appear.

⑨ Click the field header, and then choose your sort and filter options.

Note: For more information on sorting and filtering, see Chapter 4.

Customize It!

To change the way the PivotTable Field List displays, click the Field List button ([⊞ ▾]). A menu appears. You can choose from the following menu options: Field Section and Area Section Stacked, Field Section and Area Section Side by Side, Field Section Only, Area Section Only (2 by 2), and Area Section Only (1 by 4).

Modify PivotTable Data and Layout

PivotTables help you answer essential questions about your data. To extend the value of PivotTables, Excel allows you to change the data on which they are based, and the manner in which they are laid out.

PivotTables can become quite complex. Fortunately, you need not regenerate and re-edit a table every time the underlying

data changes. Instead, you can refresh a table by clicking the Refresh button.

You can easily change the layout of a PivotTable by clicking the Design tab and choosing the PivotTable style and layout you want. Excel 2007 has many pre-designed styles from which you can choose.

REFRESH DATA

① Make changes to your data.

● In this example, the data has changed here.

● There is no resulting change here.

② Click any cell in the PivotTable.

● The PivotTable Tools become available.

③ Click the Options tab.

④ Click Refresh.

● The numbers and calculations now reflect the changes in the data.

CHANGE LAYOUT

1. Click any cell in the PivotTable.

● The PivotTable Tools become available.

2. Click the Design tab.

3. Click here and select the style you want.

Excel applies the style.

4. Click to select the PivotTable style options you want.

Excel applies the options.

5. Click Report Layout.

A menu of layouts appears.

6. Click a layout.

Excel changes your report layout.

TIP

Did You Know?

By default, Excel creates or modifies your PivotTable as you click and drag fields among the Report, Column, Row Lab, and Values fields. If you do not want the PivotTable to be dynamically created or modified, click to select the Defer Layout option at the bottom of the PivotTable Field List. Click the Update button when you are ready to create or modify your PivotTable.

Compute Sub- and Grand Totals

PivotTables can automatically calculate summary statistics such as subtotals and grand totals for the columns and rows in your list. When calculating subtotals and grand totals, you have a choice of calculations from which to choose, including sum, average, count, standard deviation, minimum, and maximum.

To change the summary statistic, open the Data Field Settings dialog box and choose the type of calculation you want to use to summarize your data.

Changing the type of calculation used to generate values in a row or column can result in improperly formatted data. To remedy this, use the Number Format button in the Value Field Settings dialog box to access the number-formatting capabilities of the Format Cells dialog box.

① Click any field in your PivotTable.

The PivotTable Tools become available.

② Click Options.

③ Click Field List.

The PivotTable Field List becomes available.

④ Click the field for which you want a sub- or grand total.

A menu of options appears.

⑤ Click Value Field Settings.

The Value Field Settings dialog box appears.

⑥ Click the type of calculation you want to use to summarize your data.

⑦ Click Number Format.

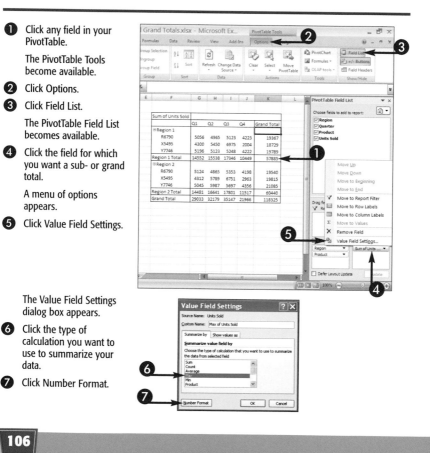

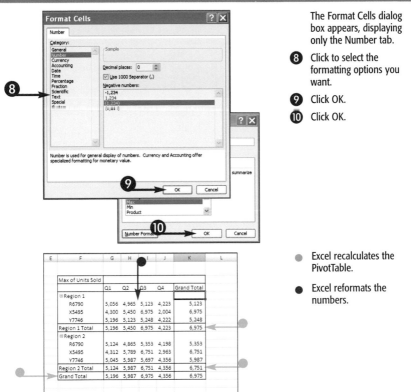

The Format Cells dialog box appears, displaying only the Number tab.

⑧ Click to select the formatting options you want.

⑨ Click OK.

⑩ Click OK.

● Excel recalculates the PivotTable.

● Excel reformats the numbers.

Change It!
In the Design tab's Layout group, click Subtotals to tell Excel whether you want to show subtotals and whether the subtotals should appear at the top or the bottom of the group. Click Grand Totals to tell Excel whether you want to show grand totals for rows and columns, just for rows, or just for columns.

Create a Calculated Field

With a PivotTable, you can create new fields, called calculated fields. You base calculated fields on the values in existing fields. You create a calculated field by performing simple arithmetic on every value in the existing field.

You commonly use calculated fields with continuous data such as incomes, prices, miles, and sales. For example, you can

multiply each value in a field called Price by a sales tax rate to create a calculated field called Tax.

To create a calculated field, use the Insert Calculated Field dialog box. Your calculated fields are available in the PivotTable Field List for use in your PivotTable. You can only use the calculated field in data cells.

① Click any field in your PivotTable.

● The PivotTable Tools become available.

② Click Options.

③ Click Field List.

The PivotTable Field List becomes available.

④ Click Formulas.

A menu appears.

⑤ Click Calculated Field.

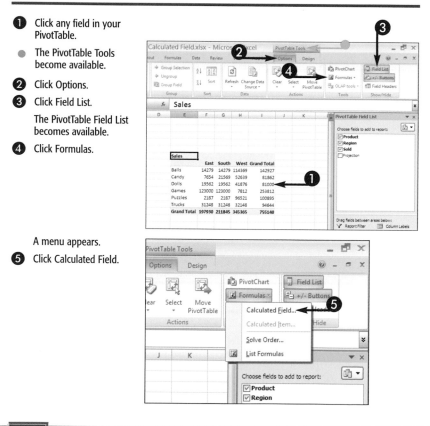

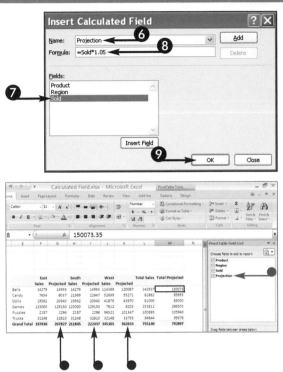

The Insert Calculated Field dialog box appears.

⑥ Type a name for the new field.

⑦ Double-click an existing field to use in defining the field.

⑧ Type an operator and the value, such as * 1.05.

⑨ Click OK.

● Values for the calculated field fill the data area.

In this example, the field name has been changed.

● The calculated field appears at the end of the field list.

Did You Know?

You can use the Data Field Settings dialog box to change the name of your field headers. Open the dialog box and type a new name in the Custom Name field. To remove field headers from your PivotTable, click the Options tab, and then click Field Headers to toggle off the field headers.

Hide Columns or Rows in a PivotTable

Grouping is a PivotTable formatting option. With Grouping, you can hide detail so that you can easily compare groups of data. When you group columns or rows, Excel totals the data, creates a field header, and creates a field with a drill-down button that displays either a plus or a minus sign.

When the drill-down button displays a minus sign, you can click the button to collapse the data. When the drill-down button displays a plus sign, you can click the button to expand the data. If you do not want to display the button, you can click the +/- buttons icon on the Options tab to toggle the display of buttons to off. After grouping your data, you can then ungroup it.

---

① Click and drag the row or column labels to select the rows or columns you want to hide.

● These are column labels.

② Click the Options tab.

③ Click Group Selection.

● A new cell appears, with a Minus button.

④ Click the Minus button.

The details of the rows or columns are hidden, the totals display, and the minus sign on the button turns into a plus sign.

● Click the Plus button to see the hidden cells again.

⑤ Click the cell that contains the group header.

⑥ Click Ungroup.

Excel removes the grouping.

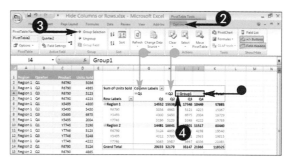

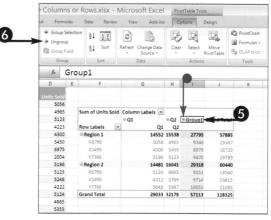

Sorting enables you to see patterns in your data. You can sort PivotTables by field labels or by data values. When you sort by field labels, Excel sorts the corresponding data values as well. The opposite is also true: Sorting the data values rearranges the field labels.

You can sort your PivotTable in either ascending or descending order. You can also specify the sort direction: top to bottom or left to right. This can become a bit confusing, so the Sort By Value dialog box provides you with an explanation of the results of your sort selection.

SORT FIELD LABELS

① Click any field in your PivotTable.

● The PivotTable Tools become available.

② Click the Options tab.

③ Drag to select the field labels you want to sort.

④ Click the ascending or descending icon.

Excel sorts your field labels.

SORT DATA FIELDS

① Click and drag to select the data you want to sort.

② Click Sort.

The Sort By Value dialog box appears.

③ Click a sort option.

④ Click a sort direction.

● The Sort By Value dialog box provides an explanation of the results of your sort selection.

⑤ Click OK.

Excel sorts your data fields.

111

Create a PivotChart

PivotCharts, which are based on PivotTables, make patterns in your data more apparent. When you create a chart from a PivotTable, you can base your chart on summary statistics, and you can adjust the row and column layout. After creating your chart, you can display the PivotTable Field List, and change the layout of your PivotTable. As you do, your PivotChart changes automatically.

PivotCharts have options that regular charts do not have. For example, you can filter the data that displays in your PivotChart. As a result, if your data is divided into multiple regions, you can easily specify which regions display in your PivotChart.

---

① Click any cell in your PivotTable.

● The PivotTable Tools become available.

② Click the Options tab.

③ Click PivotChart.

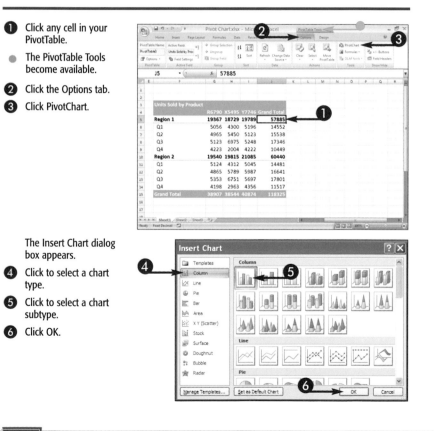

The Insert Chart dialog box appears.

④ Click to select a chart type.

⑤ Click to select a chart subtype.

⑥ Click OK.

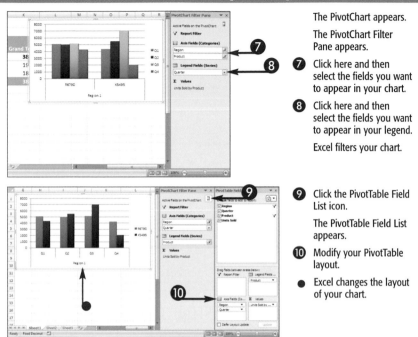

The PivotChart appears.

The PivotChart Filter Pane appears.

⑦ Click here and then select the fields you want to appear in your chart.

⑧ Click here and then select the fields you want to appear in your legend.

Excel filters your chart.

⑨ Click the PivotTable Field List icon.

The PivotTable Field List appears.

⑩ Modify your PivotTable layout.

● Excel changes the layout of your chart.

TIP

Did You Know?

To remove all the filters from your PivotChart, click your chart to activate the PivotChart Tools. Click the Options tab, click Clear, and then click Clear Filters. To clear your PivotChart and your PivotTable, click the chart to activate the PivotChart Tools, click the Options tab, click Clear, and then click Clear All.

Describe Data with Statistics

Excel includes more than 80 statistical functions. You can find these functions by using the Function Wizard in the Statistics category. Some of these functions are also available in the Descriptive Statistics dialog box. To make descriptive statistics available, you must install the Data Analysis ToolPak add-in, as described in Chapter 10.

To use descriptive statistics, first display a worksheet with the data you want to analyze. You can generate the worksheet within Excel, or import it from Access or another data source. Many functions work only with numeric data. For imported data or other data that may contain numbers in text form, see Chapter 3 to learn how to convert text to numbers.

① Click the Data tab.

② Click Data Analysis.

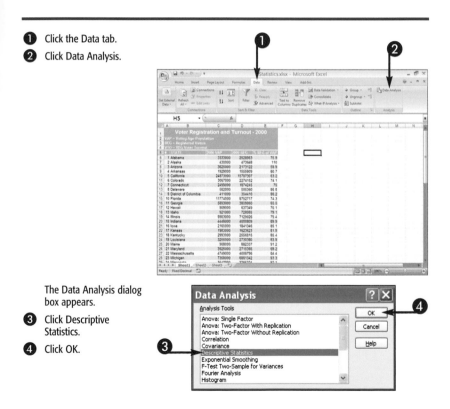

The Data Analysis dialog box appears.

③ Click Descriptive Statistics.

④ Click OK.

Descriptive Statistics `[?][X]`

Input
Input Range: `$D$5:$D$56`
Grouped By: ⊙ Columns
           ○ Rows
☑ Labels in first row

Output options
⊙ Output Range: `$H$5`
○ New Worksheet Ply:
○ New Workbook
☑ Summary statistics
☐ Confidence Level for Mean: `95` %
☐ Kth Largest: `1`
☐ Kth Smallest: `1`

`OK`
`Cancel`
`Help`

G	H	I	J
		2000 REG	
	Mean	3192271.653	
	Standard Error	462816.3518	
	Median	2173122	
	Mode	#N/A	
	Standard Deviation	3239714.463	
	Sample Variance	1.04957E+13	
	Kurtosis	4.132430428	
	Skewness	1.930224792	
	Range	15487295	
	Minimum	220012	
	Maximum	15707307	
	Sum	156421311	
	Count	49	

The Descriptive Statistics dialog box appears.

⑤ Click and drag the cells you want to describe, or type the cell range.

⑥ Click if the first row of your statistics is a label.

⑦ Click to select where you want the output to appear.

● If necessary, type a location.

⑧ Click to select the Summary statistics option.

● You can also include other statistics.

⑨ Click OK.

The statistics appear in a boxed area.

To see all of your statistics, widen the column heads by clicking the border between column letters and dragging.

TIP

Did You Know?
Descriptive statistics are available as Excel functions.

Excel Functions

Descriptive Statistic	Excel Function	Descriptive Statistic	Excel Function
Mean	AVERAGE	Median	MEDIAN
Mode	MODE	Standard Deviation	STDEV

Find the Correlation Between Variables

With a correlation, you can measure the relationship between two variables. For example, you can explore questions such as whether baseball players hit fewer home runs as they age.

You can use the CORREL function to determine a correlation. CORREL takes two arguments, array1 and array2, which are the two lists of numbers. The result of the function is a number, 'r', between –1 and 1. The closer 'r' gets to –1 or 1, the stronger the relationship. If 'r' is negative, the relationship is an inverse relationship — for example, as age increases, batting averages decrease. A positive result suggests that as one variable increases, so does the other.

---

① Click the cell in which you want to place your answer.

② Type **=CORREL(** or double-click CORREL on the function AutoComplete list.

	A	B	C	D
		2007 Sales	Years	
1	Sales Representative	($)	Employed	
2	Johnson	200,415	4	
3	Smith	300,125	3	
4	Jones	142,569	3	
5	Jefferson	509,268	1	
6	Kinkade	205,916	4	
7	Richardson	452,361	4	
8	Allen	321,210	7	
9	Briget	423,156	8	
10	Paulson	215,467	3	
11	Morris	234,567	4	
12	Total	3,005,054		
13	Correlation Between Sales and Years Employed	=CORREL(		
14				
15				
16				

NETWORKDAYS ✕ ✓ ƒx =CORREL(

CORREL(**array1**, array2)

Sheet1 Sheet2 Sheet3

Enter   Fixed Decimal

③ Click the Insert Function icon.

	A	B	C	D
		2007 Sales	Years	
1	Sales Representative	($)	Employed	
2	Johnson	200,415	4	
3	Smith	300,125	3	
4	Jones	142,569	3	

NETWORKDAYS ✕ ✓ ƒx =CORREL(

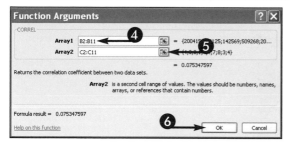

Function Arguments

CORREL

| Array1 | B2:B11 | = {20041...25;142569;509268;20... |
| Array2 | C2:C11 | = {4,3,3,7;8;3;4} |

= 0.075347597

Returns the correlation coefficient between two data sets.

Array2 is a second cell range of values. The values should be numbers, names, arrays, or references that contain numbers.

Formula result = 0.075347597

Help on this function   OK   Cancel

	A	B	C	D
1	Sales Representative	**2007 Sales ($)**	Years Employed	
2	Johnson	200,415	4	
3	Smith	300,125	3	
4	Jones	142,569	3	
5	Jefferson	509,268	1	
6	Kinkade	205,916	4	
7	Richardson	452,361	4	
8	Allen	321,210	7	
9	Briget	423,156	8	
10	Paulson	215,467	3	
11	Morris	234,567	4	
12	**Total**	**3,005,054**		
13	**Correlation Between Sales and Years Employed**	0.0753476		
14				

The Function Arguments dialog box appears.

④ Click and drag to select the first series of numbers, or type the cell range.

⑤ Click and drag to select the second series of numbers, or type the cell range.

Note: You can select a subset of a list, but make sure that the same subset is selected for each list.

⑥ Click OK.

● The correlation coefficient appears.

The sign indicates whether the relationship is positive (+) or negative (−).

Did You Know?

When using the CORREL function, if a reference cell contains text, logical values, or empty cells, Excel ignores those values. However, reference cells that have a value of zero are included in the calculation. If the number of data points in array1 and array2 are not equal, Excel returns the error message #N/A.

Explore Outcomes with What-If Analysis

When you use the PMT function, you can find out how a change in the loan amount, loan length, or interest rate — or some combination of these factors — affects the monthly payment. By typing in different amounts, rates, and periods, you can see how different scenarios affect the monthly payment.

What-if analysis is a systematic way of finding out how a change in one or more variables affects a result. The Scenario Manager feature allows you to vary one or more inputs to find out how the result changes. The advantage of the Scenario Manager is that it stores a series of values so that you can create a single report or table showing how each value or combination of values influences the result.

Note: You must first enter the values required into a worksheet and type the formula that calculates the answer. This example uses the IRR function, discussed in Chapter 2.

1 Click and drag to select the cells that contain the values you want to vary.

2 Click the Data tab.

3 Click the What-if analysis icon.

A menu appears.

4 Click Scenario Manager.

The Scenario Manager dialog box appears.

5 Click Add.

● The Add Scenario dialog box appears, indicating the cells selected in step 1.

6 Type a name for the scenario.

7 Click OK.

Scenario Values ? ☒

Enter values for each of the changing cells.

1:	Investment	-6607
2:	Payment_1	2000
3:	Payment_2	2000
4:	Payment_3	2000
5:	Payment_4	2500

Add   OK   Cancel

Scenario Manager ? ☒

Scenarios:

Scenario 1
Scenario 2
Scenario 3
Scenario 4

Add...
Delete
Edit...
Merge...
Summary...

Changing cells: $B$2:$B$6

Comment: Created by Denise Etheridge on 10/1/2006

Show   Close

Scenario Summary ? ☒

Report type
◉ Scenario summary
○ Scenario PivotTable report

Result cells:

OK   Cancel

The Scenario Values dialog box appears.

⑧ Type the scenario values.

⑨ Click Add to create more scenarios.

The Add Scenario dialog box appears. Repeat steps 6 and 7.

⑩ Click OK instead of Add when you finish.

The Scenario Manager dialog box appears.

⑪ Click Summary.

The Scenario Summary dialog box appears.

⑫ Click to select a report type.

⑬ Click the field or type the cell address of the field that calculates the results.

⑭ Click OK.

The type of report you requested appears on a new worksheet, displaying how each value affects the result.

Scenario Summary		Current Values:	Scenario 1	Scenario 2	Scenario 3	Scenario 4
Changing Cells:						
	Investment	-6607	-6607	-6607	-6607	-6607
	Payment_1	2500	2000	2500	5000	1000
	Payment_2	3000	2000	2000	1000	1000
	Payment_3	1000	2000	2000	1000	1000
	Payment_4	2000	2500	1800	1500	5000
Result Cells:						
	Interest	12.00%	10.50%	11.34%	15.12%	6.13%

Notes: Current Values column represents values of changing cells at time Scenario Summary Report was created. Changing cells for each scenario are highlighted in gray.

Did You Know?

If you name cells, your scenario summary becomes easier to read because Excel displays the cell name instead of the cell address. For example, in this task, you can name cell B2 Investment and cell B7 Interest_Earned. To learn how to name cells, see Chapter 1.

Optimize a Result with Goal Seek

Excel gives you a powerful tool for finding a way to reach your goals. For example, if you need a loan for a new home, your goal might be to pay a specific monthly payment. You can use the Goal Seek feature to show how you can reach your goal by adjusting one of the loan terms, such as the interest rate or loan amount.

You could also have Goal Seek find the interest rate required to reach your payment goal, given a loan amount, or find the loan amount required to reach your goal, given a specific interest rate.

To find specific inputs that result in a specific goal, you need to use Solver, which is an add-in. See Chapter 10 to learn more about add-ins.

---

① Click the cell that contains the value you want to reach.

② Click the Data tab.

③ Click the What-if analysis icon.

A menu appears.

④ Click Goal Seek.

	A	B
1	Principal	$120,000
2	Interest	5.00%
3	Number of Months	180
4	Monthly Payments	($948.95)
5		

The Goal Seek dialog box appears.

⑤ Type the value you want to reach.

⑥ Click or type the cell address of the cell whose value you want to change to reach your goal.

⑦ Click OK.

Monthly_Pa... =PMT(B2/12,Number_of_Months,Principal)

	A	B
1	Principal	$120,000
2	Interest	5.00%
3	Number of Months	180
4	Monthly Payments	($9...5)
5		
6		

Goal Seek
Set cell: B4
To value: -900
By changing cell: $B$2

B4	▾	fx	=PMT(B2/12,Number_of_Months,Principal)

	A	B	C	D	E	F	G	H
1	Principal	$120,000		Goal Seek Status	? X			
2	Interest	4.20%		Goal Seeking with Cell B4 found a solution.	Step			
3	Number of Months	180		Target value: -900	Pause			
4	Monthly Payments	($900.00)		Current value: ($900.00)				
5				OK	Cancel			
6								

B4	▾	fx	=PMT(B2/12,Number_ **8** Months,Principal)

	A	B	C	D	E	F	G	H
1	Principal	$113,810 ◄						
2	Interest	5.00%		Goal Seek Status	? X			
3	Number of Months	180		Goal Seeking with Cell B4 found a solution.	Step			
4	Monthly Payments	($900.00)		Target value: -900	Pause			
5				Current value: ($900.00)				
6				OK	Cancel			

The Goal Seek status dialog box appears.

● The result appears in the worksheet.

8 Click OK to accept the change.

● Alternatively, you can click Cancel to restore the original values.

In this example, the principal is kept the same, and the $900 monthly payment can be reached by finding an interest rate of 4.2 percent.

Repeat steps 1 to 7 for another value.

● In this example, the interest is kept the same, and the $900 monthly payment can be reached by decreasing the principal to $113,810.

Did You Know?

The example in this task shows the loan amount required to bring the monthly payment down to $900, in this case $113,810. You would need to contribute a down payment of just over $6,000 to bring the loan down to that amount. You could construct a worksheet that allows you to enter various down-payment amounts.

Creating Charts

Excel gives you tools for quickly generating a chart, or visual representation, of the numbers in your worksheet. Charts clarify patterns that can get lost in rows and columns of numbers, and they make your data more accessible to people who are not familiar with, or do not want to delve into, the details.

Charts can make a greater impression than rows and columns of numbers because the mind perceives, processes, and recalls visual information more quickly than textual or numerical information. In addition, shapes and colors have real impact. This effectiveness, however, can be a liability when charts emphasize unimportant or misleading patterns. This chapter helps you

become comfortable with the Excel charting tools, so you can communicate your content as effectively as possible.

In this chapter, you find out how to generate a chart quickly. You then learn how to add chart details, change the chart type, and remove data series. One task shows you how to create a trendline. A trendline visually summarizes the direction and magnitude of change over time.

Anyone who uses Excel to manage and analyze experimental data can benefit from the section on error bars. Several tasks provide special insights – for example, the section on histograms shows you how to plot frequencies.

Quick Tips

Create a Chart That Has Visual Appeal 124

Add Chart Details 126

Change the Chart Type 130

Add a Trendline to a Chart 132

Add and Remove Chart Data 134

Add Error Bars 136

Create a Histogram 138

Create a Chart That Has Visual Appeal

With Excel 2007, you can quickly and easily create charts with dramatic visual appeal. Simply select the data you want to chart, and then choose a chart type from the Insert tab's Charts group.

After you create your chart, Excel makes Chart Tools available to you through the Design, Layout, and Format contextual tabs. By using the Chart Tools, you can choose a chart style and layout. You can change the color scheme of your chart with chart styles and use layouts to add a chart title, axis labels, a legend, or a data table to your chart.

---

① Click and drag to select the worksheet data you want to chart.

Include row and column headings.

② Click the Insert tab.

③ Click a chart type.

④ Click a chart subtype.

Excel creates a chart based on the data you selected.

● The Chart Tools become available.

⑤ Click the Design tab.

⑥ Click here and select a chart style.

Excel applies the style to your chart.

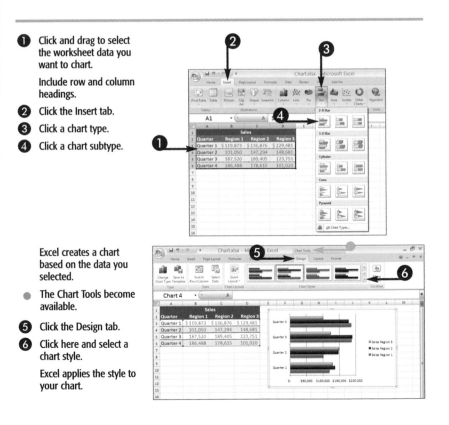

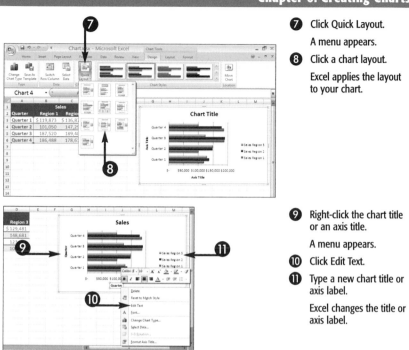

⑦ Click Quick Layout.

A menu appears.

⑧ Click a chart layout.

Excel applies the layout to your chart.

⑨ Right-click the chart title or an axis title.

A menu appears.

⑩ Click Edit Text.

⑪ Type a new chart title or axis label.

Excel changes the title or axis label.

TIP

Did You Know?
The fastest way to create a chart using Excel's charting defaults is to select the data that you want to chart, and then press F11. Excel creates a chart on a new worksheet. You can then modify the chart by using any of the Chart Tools.

Add Chart Details

After you create your chart, Excel makes it easy for you to modify it or add more details. In fact, you can modify virtually all the elements of a chart.

When you create a chart, Excel places it on the same worksheet as the data from which you created it. You can then move the chart to another worksheet or to a special chart sheet.

To make a 3-D chart easier to read, you can use the X and Y fields in the Format Chart Area dialog box to change the chart rotation. In addition to changing your chart's rotation, you may also want to change its perspective.

CHANGE CHART LOCATION

① Click your chart.

● The Chart Tools become available.

② Click the Design tab.

③ Click Move Chart.

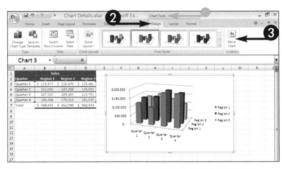

The Move Chart dialog box appears.

④ Click to select the New sheet option.

● Alternatively, click Object in to place the chart on another sheet.

● Click here and select the sheet on which you want to place the chart.

⑤ Type a name for the sheet.

⑥ Click OK.

Excel places the chart on a chart sheet or another worksheet.

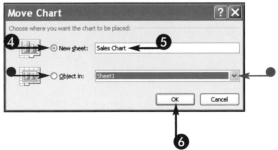

**CHANGE ROTATION
AND PERSPECTIVE**

① Click the Layout tab.

② Click 3-D Rotation.

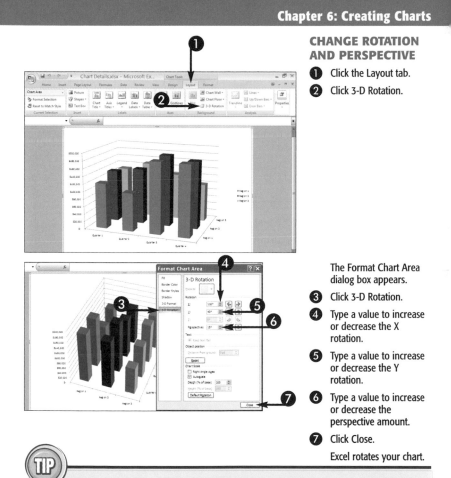

The Format Chart Area
dialog box appears.

③ Click 3-D Rotation.

④ Type a value to increase
or decrease the X
rotation.

⑤ Type a value to increase
or decrease the Y
rotation.

⑥ Type a value to increase
or decrease the
perspective amount.

⑦ Click Close.

Excel rotates your chart.

TIP

Did You Know?
You can edit any element in your chart by right-clicking it. A menu
appears, sometimes with a mini-toolbar. Use the menu and mini-toolbar
to add or delete elements, to change the font, to change the font size, to
change the alignment, or to edit the data source.

continued

To make your chart more readable, you may want to change some of its attributes. For example, you can easily change the walls and floor of your three-dimensional charts. The walls are the side and back of your chart, and the floor is the bottom of your chart.

Excel bases Axis values on the range of values in your data. Axis values encompass the range. Axis labels describe the data displayed on each axis. Excel provides several options for choosing whether and how to display the axis values and labels on each axis. These options include the horizontal, vertical, and depth axis.

CHANGE THE WALL AND FLOOR

① Click your chart.

● The Chart Tools become available.

② Click the Layout tab.

③ Click Chart Wall.

A menu appears.

④ Click More Wall Options.

● Alternatively, choose an option from the menu.

The Format Walls dialog box appears.

⑤ Click Fill.

⑥ Click to choose a fill option.

● Set any additional options.

⑦ Click Close.

Excel changes the fill of the chart wall.

To change the chart floor, you can click Chart Floor and then repeat steps 2 to 6.

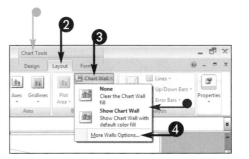

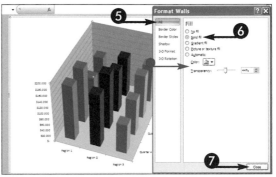

ADJUST THE AXIS

1 Click the Layout tab.

2 Click Axes.

3 Click Primary Horizontal Axis.

A menu appears.

4 Click a Primary Horizontal Axis option.

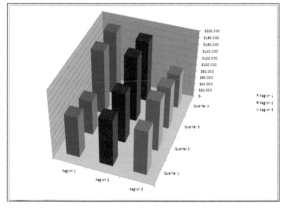

Excel changes the display of your horizontal axis.

To change the vertical axis, you can click Primary Vertical Axis.

To change the depth axis, you can click Depth Axis.

TIP

Did You Know?

You can resize a chart by clicking it. A border surrounds it, with dots on the sides and corners. Place the cursor over the dots. When a double arrow appears, click and drag to resize the chart. Be careful when resizing, because resizing may skew the chart and distort the presentation of the content.

Change the Chart Type

Excel provides a variety of chart types and subtypes from which to choose. You should choose the chart type that best represents your data.

You can use a column or bar chart to plot data arranged in rows and columns. Area and line charts are also good for plotting data organized into columns and rows. You can use an area chart to show how values change over time and how each part of the whole contributes to the change.

Line charts are ideal for showing trends in your data. Pie charts are useful when you want to display data that is arranged in one column or one row. Each data point in a pie chart represents a percentage of the whole pie.

---

① Click your chart.

● The Chart Tools become available.

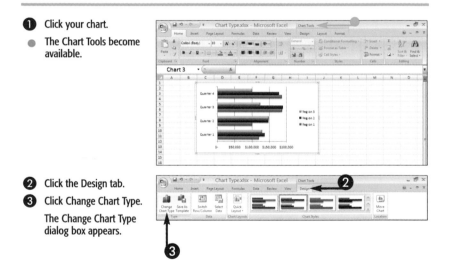

② Click the Design tab.

③ Click Change Chart Type.

The Change Chart Type dialog box appears.

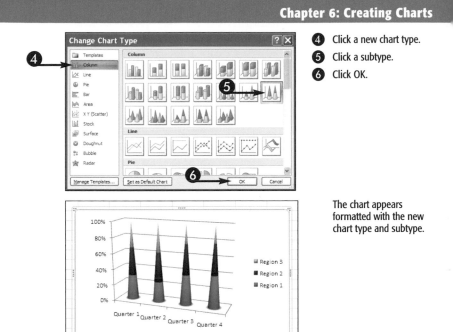

④ Click a new chart type.

⑤ Click a subtype.

⑥ Click OK.

The chart appears formatted with the new chart type and subtype.

TIP

Did You Know?

If you show more than two data series in a single chart, you can change the chart type for one or more series and create a combination chart. By using different chart types, you can make it easier to distinguish different categories of data that appear in the same chart.

Add a Trendline to a Chart

With Excel, you can add trendlines to your charts. Trendlines help you see both the size and direction of changes in your data, and you can use them to forecast future or past values, based on available data.

Excel superimposes the trendline over your chart. A trendline is the one line through your data series that is as close as possible to every point in the data series. Excel provides several trendline types. You should base the type of trendline you choose on the type of data you have.

Excel generates a statistic called R-squared that indicates how well a given trendline fits your data. The closer R-squared is to 1, the better the line fits your data.

1 Click your chart.

● The Chart Tools become available.

2 Click the Layout tab.

3 Click Trendline.

   A menu appears.

4 Click More Trendline Options.

   Alternatively, click a menu option to choose the type of trendline you want to apply.

   The Format Trendline dialog box appears.

5 Click Trendline Options.

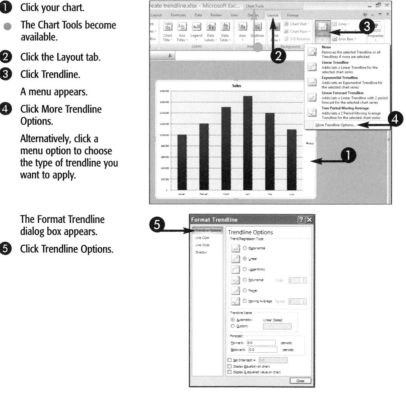

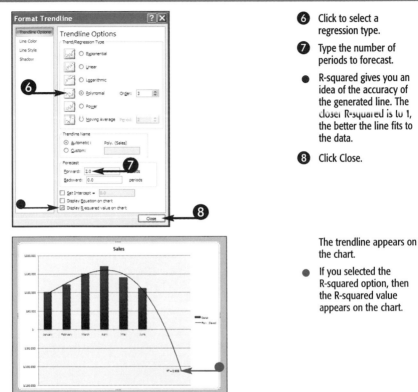

⑥ Click to select a regression type.

⑦ Type the number of periods to forecast.

● R-squared gives you an idea of the accuracy of the generated line. The closer R-squared is to 1, the better the line fits to the data.

⑧ Click Close.

The trendline appears on the chart.

● If you selected the R-squared option, then the R-squared value appears on the chart.

TIP

Did You Know?

You can project values that fit a straight-line trend by using the TREND function. You can project values that fit an exponential trend by using the GROWTH function.

Add and Remove Chart Data

If you want to include new data in your chart, or exclude data from your chart, you can use the Select Data Source dialog box. For example, you can add and remove entire columns or rows of information, or you can change your data series entirely without changing your chart's type or other properties.

You can also add to the data area of an existing data series. Use the Select Data Source dialog box's Legend Entries (Series) section to select the cell addresses that define your data series label and your data series. You can also use the Legend Entry (Series) section to add or remove a data series. If you need to switch your column and row data, then you can click the Switch Column/Row button.

CHANGE THE DATA AREA

If the chart is on the worksheet, position it so that it does not overlap the data.

● Currently charted data.

❶ Click your chart.

● The Chart Tools become available.

❷ Click the Design tab.

❸ Click Select Data.

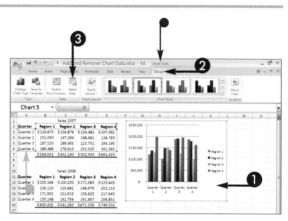

The Select Data Source dialog box appears.

❹ Click and drag to select the data you want to include in your chart, or type the cell range.

❺ Click OK.

Excel redefines the data series area.

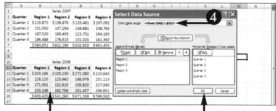

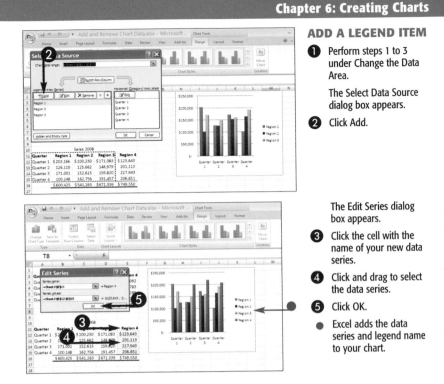

ADD A LEGEND ITEM

① Perform steps 1 to 3 under Change the Data Area.

The Select Data Source dialog box appears.

② Click Add.

The Edit Series dialog box appears.

③ Click the cell with the name of your new data series.

④ Click and drag to select the data series.

⑤ Click OK.

● Excel adds the data series and legend name to your chart.

TIP

Apply It!

Here is a quick way to add data to a chart. Click and drag to select the data you want to include in the chart. Click the Copy icon on the Home tab. Click the chart to select it, and then click the Paste icon on the Home tab. The chart reflects the added data series.

With Excel, you can easily generate error bars to provide an estimate of the potential error in experimental or sampled data. In fields such as science, marketing, and polling, people make conclusions about a population by sampling the population or devising controlled experiments.

When you sample data or generated it in laboratory conditions, the resulting

numbers approximate the larger reality you are exploring. An error bar shows the range of possible values for these experimentally derived numbers.

With Excel, you can show error bars in several ways: as a fixed number, measured in the same units used to measure data, above or below each data point in your data series; as a percentage of the data point; or in terms of standard deviation units.

① Click your chart.

● The Chart tools become available.

② Click the Layout tab.

③ Click Error Bars.

A menu appears.

④ Click More Error Bars Options.

● Alternatively, click the appropriate menu option.

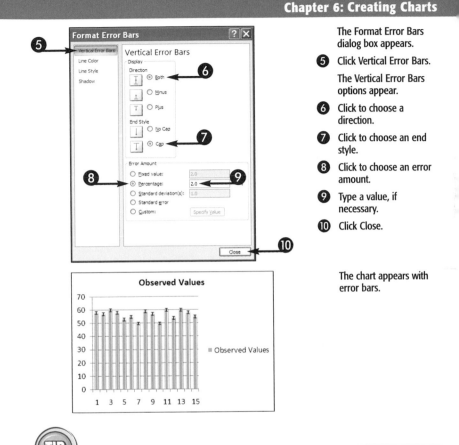

The Format Error Bars dialog box appears.

⑤ Click Vertical Error Bars.

The Vertical Error Bars options appear.

⑥ Click to choose a direction.

⑦ Click to choose an end style.

⑧ Click to choose an error amount.

⑨ Type a value, if necessary.

⑩ Click Close.

The chart appears with error bars.

TIP

Did You Know?
You can add trendlines and error bars to a PivotChart. However, if you make changes to your PivotChart, Excel may remove the trendlines or error bars. Changes that may result in the loss of trendlines or error bars include changing the layout, removing fields, and hiding or displaying items.

You can use histograms to group a list of values into categories. Excel calls these categories bins. To display the prices of different cereals, for example, your first bin might be <3, representing prices under $3.00 per box, your second bin 3.01–4.00, and so on up to a bin for all boxes priced at over $5.00. Excel counts the number of occurrences in each bin.

When creating a histogram, you must provide three pieces of information. First, define the raw data you want to sort. Then define the bins. Finally, specify the cell in which you want the result to appear.

The histogram tool is part of the Analysis ToolPak, which you may need to install as explained in Chapter 10.

---

❶ Type the values that define the bins.

Note: *The bins must be ordered from lowest to highest, although they need not be the same size.*

❷ Click the Data tab.

❸ Click Data Analysis.

The Data Analysis dialog box appears.

❹ Click Histogram.

❺ Click OK.

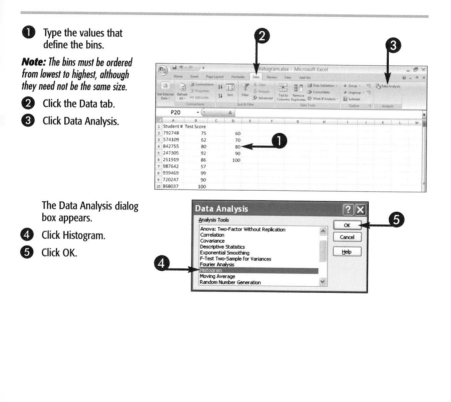

The Histogram dialog box appears.

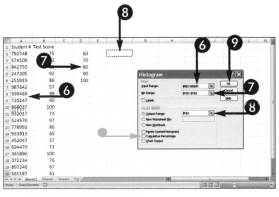

⑥ Click and drag the range of numbers to categorize, or type the cell range.

⑦ Click and drag the range of bins created in step **1**, or type the cell range.

⑧ Click the cell where you want the results to start, or type the cell range.

● You can also select other options.

⑨ Click OK.

The results appear on the same worksheet as the original data.

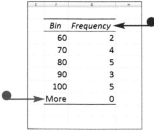

Bin	Frequency
60	2
70	4
80	5
90	3
100	5
More	0

● *Frequency* means the number of values per bin.

● *More* refers to the uncategorized values in the highest bin.

You can edit the histogram.

TIP

Did You Know?
The FREQUENCY function gives you the same capabilities as the Histogram tool. However, when you use the FREQUENCY function, Excel automatically updates your bins as you update your data.

Presenting Worksheets

You can use Excel's formatting options to adjust almost every aspect of how your worksheets appear. Formatting results in more than just making text bold or coloring cells blue. Formatting makes your worksheets easier to read and understand and thus, more useful to others.

This chapter provides tips on formatting. You learn how to apply formats quickly with Format Painter. Format Painter speeds your work because, in just a few clicks, you can copy a format from one cell to other cells.

As you probably know, Excel gives you several tools to simplify the work of formatting. The Home tab and the Format Cells dialog box provide all the controls you

need to change the look and properties of both cells and numbers. You can adjust the color, alignment, and numerous other cell properties.

With shapes, text boxes, and pictures, Excel goes even further, giving you the ability to integrate graphics into your worksheet. You can use shapes to create flow charts and other types of business graphics. Excel also supplies prepackaged styles you can apply to your graphics to give them a distinctive flair.

You can place background images behind your data, to get people's attention and perhaps to enhance the content itself. You can also take a picture of your worksheet and use the graphic in Excel or another software product.

Format Quickly with Format Painter 142

Insert Shapes into a Worksheet 144

Insert Text Boxes into a Worksheet 146

Insert Photographs into a Worksheet 148

Arrange the Graphics in a Worksheet 150

Insert a Background Image 152

Take a Picture of a Worksheet 154

Format Quickly with Format Painter

Excel can save you time when you need to reapply formats that already exist in your worksheet. The easiest way to apply a cell's format to another cell or to a range of cells is by using the Format Painter. You can use the Format Painter for one-time copying of formats within a workbook.

You can find the Format Painter tool on the Home tab in the Clipboard group. The Format Painter icon is shaped like a brush. Excel applies formats instantly. Use the Format Painter to copy and apply both cell and number formats. If you make a mistake, you can undo the formats by pressing Ctrl+Z or you can click the undo button in the Quick Access Toolbar.

 Click and drag to select cells with the format you want to copy.

Open multiple windows to see different parts of the worksheet at the same time.

Note: *See Chapter 10 to learn how to open multiple windows.*

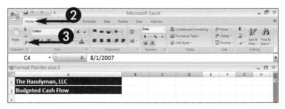

② Click the Home tab.

③ Click the Format Painter icon.

To apply the format you selected in step 1 multiple times, you can double-click the Format Painter icon.

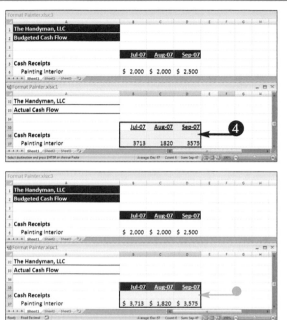

④ Click the cell in which you want to duplicate the format.

You can also click and drag to select a range of cells you want to format.

● The cell or range of cells instantly takes on the formatting of the original cell.

Apply It!

You can use the Format Painter feature to transfer properties from one image, such as clip art, to another image. The properties you transfer include background color and text flow around the image. Click the formatted picture, click the Format Painter icon, and then click the picture you want to format.

Insert Shapes into a Worksheet

Excel provides a variety of shapes, including lines, rectangles, arrows, flowchart elements, stars, banners, and callouts — all of which you can use in your worksheet. Shapes have a variety of purposes. For example, arrows point out relationships between data, and flowchart elements convey the structure of your data.

You can rotate, resize, move, and reshape shapes. You can also apply predefined styles to your shapes. Excel provides many predefined styles from which to choose.

In many cases, you can add text to your shape. You can reformat the text on your shape and change its font, size, color, and alignment. You simply select the text and then click commands on the Home tab to make your changes.

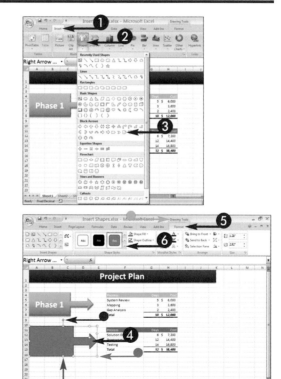

① Click the Insert tab.

② Click Shapes.

   A menu of shapes appears.

③ Click the shape that you want to add.

④ Click and drag to add the shape to your worksheet.

● The Drawing Tools become available.

● Click and drag to rotate the shape.

● Click and drag to adjust the size.

● Click and drag to adjust the size.

⑤ Click the Format tab.

⑥ Click here and select a style.

Excel formats your shape.

7 Click your shape and type your text.

8 Click and drag to the left to select your text.

9 Click the Home tab.

● Click here to adjust the size of your text.

● Click here to align your text.

● Click here to format your text.

● Click here to change the color of your text.

Excel applies your changes.

Right Arrow ...

Formula Bar

Project Plan

Process	Days	Cost
System Review	5	$ 6,000
Mapping	3	3,600
Gap Analysis	2	2,400
Total	10	$ 12,000

Phase 1

Phase 2

Process	Days	Cost
Solution Design	6	$ 7,200
Programming	12	14,400
Testing	14	16,800
Total	32	$ 38,400

Q23

Project Plan

Process	Days	Cost
System Review	5	$ 6,000
Mapping	3	3,600
Gap Analysis	2	2,400
Total	10	$ 12,000

Phase 1

Phase 2

Process	Days	Cost
Solution Design	6	$ 7,200
Programming	12	14,400
Testing	14	16,800
Total	32	$ 38,400

TIP

Apply It!
You can copy and paste shapes. Click the Home tab, click the Copy icon (⬚), and click Paste. In the menu that appears, click Paste Special. The Paste Special Dialog box appears. In the As box, click Microsoft Office Drawing Object and then click OK. A copy of your shape appears in your worksheet.

Insert Text Boxes into a Worksheet

By using a text graphic, you can create logos, add text to pictures, or add text to your worksheet. You can create text with shadows, reflections, glows, bevels, 3-D rotations, and transforms. For each option, you can choose from several sub-options, and you can apply multiple options to the same piece of text.

As with all graphics, you can resize, rotate, and reposition text boxes. You can also change the font size, alignment, and format of the text by applying the same methods used to change text that you add to a shape.

① Click the Insert tab.

② Click Text Box.

③ Click and drag to create a text box.

Your text box appears.

● The Drawing Tools become available.

④ Type your text.

⑤ Click the Format tab.

⑥ Click the Text Effects icon.

A menu appears.

⑦ Click to view the submenu for the text effects you want to apply.

⑧ Click a text effect.

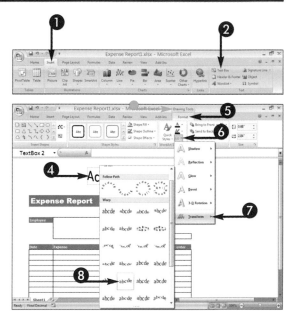

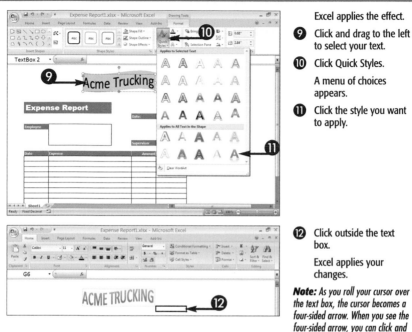

Excel applies the effect.

9 Click and drag to the left to select your text.

10 Click Quick Styles.

A menu of choices appears.

11 Click the style you want to apply.

12 Click outside the text box.

Excel applies your changes.

Note: *As you roll your cursor over the text box, the cursor becomes a four-sided arrow. When you see the four-sided arrow, you can click and drag to reposition your text.*

TIP

Did You Know?

You can use WordArt to create a text graphic. Click the Insert tab, and then click WordArt. In the list of options that appears, click the text style that you want. A text box appears with text. Press Shift+Home to select the text, type your text, and press Enter. You can modify the WordArt text just as you would any other text box.

Insert Photographs into a Worksheet

Photographs enhance your worksheet and emphasize your message. You can easily add a photograph to an Excel worksheet by locating the photograph and inserting it.

Excel has many picture styles that you can apply. You can use these styles to angle; add borders, shadows, and reflections; and otherwise stylize your photograph. As you roll your cursor over the various picture styles, Excel provides a preview of how the style appears when applied.

You can change the color of your photo's border and adjust your photo's brightness and contrast. You can even crop your photo to show only a portion of it.

In Excel, you manipulate your photographs in the same way that you manipulate any other graphic. For example, you can move them, rotate them, and resize them.

---

① Click the Insert tab.

② Click Picture.

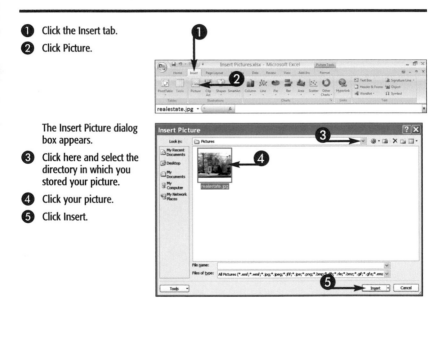

The Insert Picture dialog box appears.

③ Click here and select the directory in which you stored your picture.

④ Click your picture.

⑤ Click Insert.

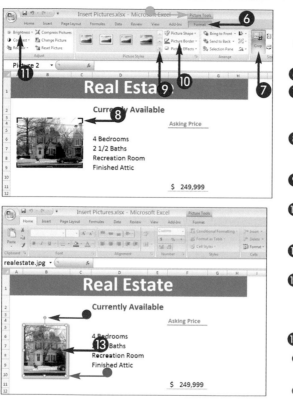

The picture appears in your worksheet.

● The Picture Tools become available.

6 Click the Format tab.

7 Click Crop.

Black markings appear on your photo.

8 Click and drag the markings to crop your photo.

9 Click here and select a picture style.

10 Click here and select a color for your picture's border.

11 Click here and select a brightness adjustment.

12 Click outside of your photo.

Excel applies the options that you selected.

13 Click your photo.

● You can click and drag to rotate the photo.

● You can click and drag to resize the photo.

TIP

Did You Know?
You can use Excel to colorize your photographs. Click your photo, click the Format tab, and then click Recolor. Among other choices, you can change your photo to grayscale or to a sepia tone.

Arrange the Graphics in a Worksheet

When you place a shape, text box, picture, clip art, or any other type of graphic in your Excel worksheet, Excel stacks it. When graphics overlap, graphics that are higher in the stack appear to be on top of graphics that are lower in the stack. This can cause problems. For example, the text you want to place on a photograph could actually appear behind the photograph.

Fortunately, you can change the stacking order. You can use the Selection and Visibility pane to choose the exact stack order in which your graphics display.

Excel also provides tools to help you arrange graphics on your worksheet. You can select graphics and then align or rotate them.

---

① Click a graphic.

● The Drawing Tools become available.

② Click the Format tab.

③ Click Selection Pane.

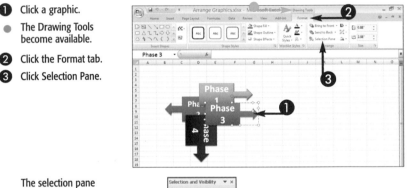

The selection pane appears.

④ Double-click a shape name and type a new name.

⑤ Click here to reorder the graphics.

● You can click here to move the graphics up.

● You can click here to move the graphics down.

⑥ Click here to hide graphics.

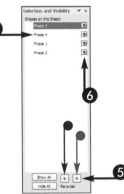

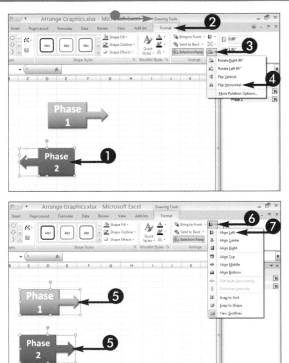

ROTATE AND ALIGN GRAPHICS

① Click a graphic to select it.

● The Drawing Tools become available.

② Click the Format tab.

③ Click the Rotate icon.

A menu appears.

④ Click to select a rotation option.

Excel rotates your graphic.

⑤ Hold down the Shift key and click to select the objects you want to align.

⑥ Click the Align icon.

A menu appears.

⑦ Click to select an alignment option.

Excel aligns your graphics.

TIP

Did You Know?

You can group your graphics. Grouping graphics allows you to treat two or more graphics as if they were one. As you move one graphic, all the other graphics in the same group move with it. To group graphics, hold down the Shift key and click each graphic that you want to group. Click the Format tab, then click the Group icon (⊞▾), and then click Group.

Insert a Background Image

Placing a background image behind a worksheet can enhance the appearance of otherwise drab columns of numbers. For example, by using a company logo, you can convey official status. Backgrounds can also create a dramatic or decorative effect that relates to worksheet content.

A background shows a color or image under the text and covers the entire surface of the worksheet. You can use

images in any standard format, such as JPG, BMP, PNG, or GIF. Excel tiles your worksheet with the image.

If you are including your worksheet in a presentation, you may want to view it in Full Screen mode. Keep in mind that when you print your worksheet or publish your worksheet as a Web page, the image is not printed or displayed on the Web page.

---

① Click the Page Layout tab.

② Click Background.

The Sheet Background dialog box appears.

③ Click here and select the folder in which you stored your image.

④ Click your image.

⑤ Click Insert.

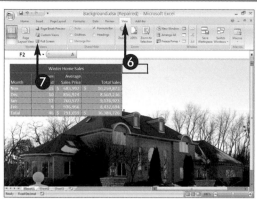

The image appears in your worksheet.

You can click Delete Background on the Page Layout tab to remove the image.

⑥ Click View.

⑦ Click Full Screen.

Your worksheet displays in Full Screen mode.

Note: Press Esc to return to Normal mode.

TIP

Did You Know?

If you do not want to see the formula bar, headings, or gridlines when you present your worksheet, then you can hide them. Click the View tab and then click Show/Hide. A menu of options appears. Deselect the options you want to hide.

Take a Picture of a Worksheet

You can take snapshots of cell ranges in your worksheet by using Excel's Copy as Picture feature. The Copy as Picture feature turns whatever you copy into a graphic you can manipulate just as you would any other graphic. In fact, you can apply styles, shapes, borders, and picture effects to your graphic. You can also adjust its brightness and contrast, and you can recolor it.

You can copy your graphic to the Clipboard and paste it into other office products such as Word, or nonoffice products such as Photoshop. Using the Copy as Picture feature is as simple as copying and pasting.

1 Click and drag to select cells.

2 Click the Home tab.

3 Click Paste.

A menu appears.

4 Click As Picture.

5 Click Copy as Picture.

The Copy Picture dialog box appears.

6 Click As shown on screen.

7 Click Picture.

8 Click OK.

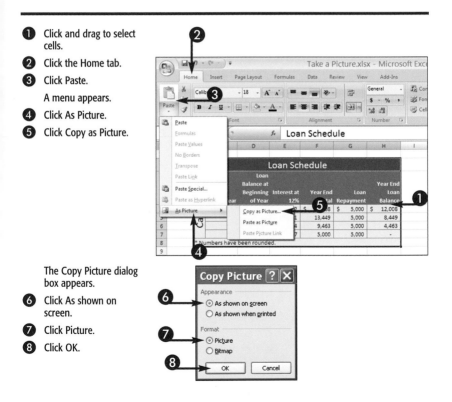

9️⃣ Click the location where you want to paste the picture.

🔟 Click Paste.

A menu appears.

1️⃣1️⃣ Click As Picture.

1️⃣2️⃣ Click Paste as Picture.

Excel pastes the cells as a picture.

● The Picture Tools become available.

TIP

Did You Know?

You can add the Camera icon (📷) to the Quick Access toolbar and use it to take pictures of your worksheet. You select the cells, click the Camera icon, and then click the location where you want to paste the picture. You cannot use the Picture Tools with graphics that you create with the Camera icon. See Chapter 10 to learn how to add an icon to the Quick Access toolbar.

Protecting, Saving, and Printing

After you complete the work of entering, analyzing, charting, and formatting your data, you can share it with others. Sharing data generally means saving it and then sharing either the file or the printout.

The tips in this chapter make it easier to share your work with others. The chapter starts by teaching you how to protect your worksheet so others can view and print it but cannot make changes to it. Next, you learn how to save a workbook as a template. By saving a workbook as a template, you eliminate the chore of re-creating a special-purpose worksheet each time you need to use it.

You can save documents in many formats. In this chapter, we review a few formats and explain the advantages of each.

The printing tips in this chapter focus on printing multiple areas of a worksheet and multiple sheets from a workbook. When printing multiple areas, you learn how to select noncontiguous cell ranges and print them, and how to repeat row and column labels across several pages.

Two key printing tools are the Page Setup dialog box and the Print Preview window. You should spend time familiarizing yourself with the many choices they offer.

Chapter 9 carries forward the themes introduced in this chapter. There you learn how to publish interactive spreadsheets on the Web, as well as how to exchange data between Excel and other applications.

Quick Tips

Protect a Worksheet...158

Save a Workbook as a Template 160

Choose a Format When Saving a Workbook..162

Print Multiple Areas of a Worksheet...164

Print Multiple Worksheets from a Workbook 166

Protect a Worksheet

If you share your worksheets with others, you can protect them so that others can view and print them, but cannot make changes. Even if you do not share your worksheets, you may want to lock certain areas so that you do not inadvertently make changes. Locking your worksheet enables you to make certain types of changes while disallowing others.

By default, when you lock a worksheet, Excel locks every cell in the worksheet, and the formulas are visible to anyone who uses the worksheet. You can specify cells that will remain unlocked, and you can hide formulas.

To protect your worksheet, you can enter a password. However, if you forget your password, you will no longer be able to access the locked areas.

---

① Click and drag to select the cells you want to remain unlocked or whose formulas you want to hide.

② Click the Home tab.

③ Click Format.

A menu appears.

④ Click Format Cells.

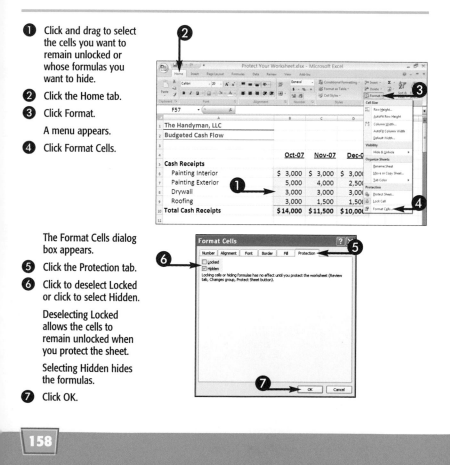

The Format Cells dialog box appears.

⑤ Click the Protection tab.

⑥ Click to deselect Locked or click to select Hidden.

Deselecting Locked allows the cells to remain unlocked when you protect the sheet.

Selecting Hidden hides the formulas.

⑦ Click OK.

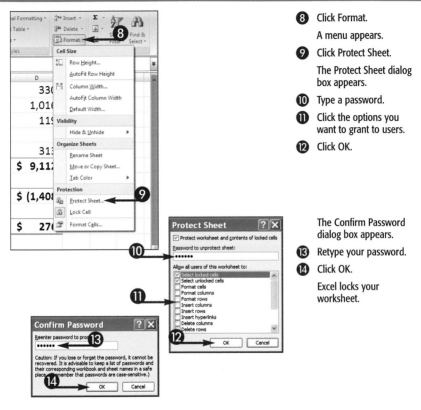

8 Click Format.

A menu appears.

9 Click Protect Sheet.

The Protect Sheet dialog box appears.

10 Type a password.

11 Click the options you want to grant to users.

12 Click OK.

The Confirm Password dialog box appears.

13 Retype your password.

14 Click OK.

Excel locks your worksheet.

TIP

Did You Know?

If you click the Review tab and then click Allow Users to Edit Ranges, the Allow Users to Edit Ranges dialog box appears. You can use this dialog box to specify the ranges that users can modify. Click the New button and type a title and the cells users can modify. You can separately password-protect each range you allow.

Save a Workbook as a Template

Templates are special-purpose workbooks you use to create new worksheets. They can contain formats, styles, and specific content such as images, column heads, and date ranges you want to reuse in other worksheets.

Excel worksheets ordinarily have the .xlsx file extension. Saving an Excel worksheet as a template creates a file with the .xltx file extension.

To use a template you have created, you can click the Microsoft Office button and then click New. In the New Workbook dialog box that appears, double-click My templates. In the New dialog box that appears, click the template you want to open and then click OK. Excel opens your template. When you save your modified file, save it as a regular file with an .xlsx file extension so that you do not overwrite your original file.

---

① Open the workbook you want to use as a template.

Templates can consist of actual data, column labels, and empty cells, with specific number formats such as percentage.

② Click the Microsoft Office button.

A menu appears.

③ Click Save As.

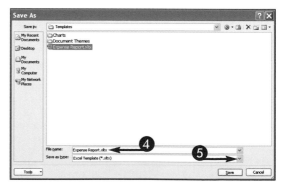

The Save As dialog box appears.

④ Type a name for your template.

⑤ Click here and select Excel Template (*.xltx).

- The Save in folder changes to Templates.

- The file extension changes to .xltx.

6 Click Save.

- Excel creates the template.

TIP

Did You Know?

Excel comes with ready-made templates that serve basic business purposes such as invoicing. To open and use one of these templates, click the Microsoft Office button and then click New. The New Workbook dialog box appears. Click Installed Templates. Click the template that you want to open, and then click Create.

Choose a Format when Saving a Workbook

After you create a Microsoft Excel 2007 worksheet, you may want to share it with others. The file format you choose when you save your file can help you. The default format for Office 2007 is Excel Workbook (*.xlsx). It creates smaller files that are easily accessible in other software programs because the files are in XML format.

Previous versions of Excel did not use XML as the default format. These files have an .xls file extension. If you want to share your documents with people who use Excel 97 to 2003, you can save your file in the Excel 97-2003 workbook (*.xls) format.

You can also save your worksheet in other file formats, including several text-based formats such as Text (Tab — delimited).

① Click the Microsoft Office button.

A menu appears.

② Click Save As.

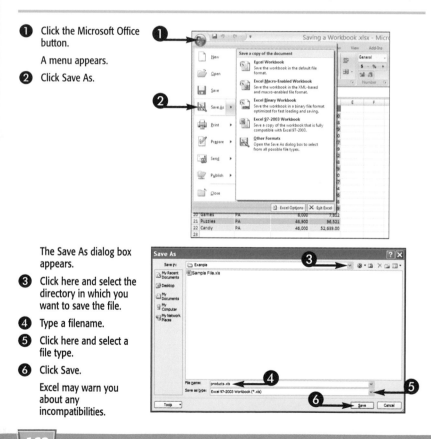

The Save As dialog box appears.

③ Click here and select the directory in which you want to save the file.

④ Type a filename.

⑤ Click here and select a file type.

⑥ Click Save.

Excel may warn you about any incompatibilities.

Excel saves your worksheet.

This example saves the file in a format that is compatible with Office 2003.

This example shows a file that is saved in CSV format.

TIP

Did You Know?

If you have a computer with Excel 97 to 2003 installed, you can go to the Office Update Website and download the 2007 Microsoft Office system Compatibility Pack for Excel. Once you install the Compatibility Pack, you can open Excel 2007 files in Excel 97 to 2003. Recent Excel features and formatting may not display in the earlier version, but they will still be available when you open the file again in Excel 2007.

Print Multiple Areas of a Worksheet

You can print noncontiguous areas of your worksheet, thereby limiting your printing to the information that is relevant.

There are many reasons why you may want to print noncontiguous areas of your worksheet. For example, if you have sales data for several products, each in a column, you can select and print only the columns in which you are interested.

When printing noncontiguous areas, you may have column headings or row labels you want to print with each selection. You can specify the rows you want to repeat at the top, or the columns you want to repeat down the left side of every page you print.

When you print a worksheet with multiple selected areas, each area prints on its own page.

---

1. Hold down the Ctrl key as you click and drag to select each area you want to print.

2. Click the Page Layout tab.

3. Click Print Area.

4. Click Set Print Area.

5. Click Print Titles.

The Page Setup dialog box appears.

6. Click the Sheet tab.

7. Click and drag the columns or rows you want to repeat or type the range.

8. Click Print Preview.

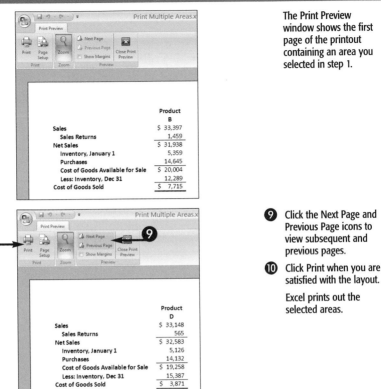

The Print Preview window shows the first page of the printout containing an area you selected in step 1.

⑨ Click the Next Page and Previous Page icons to view subsequent and previous pages.

⑩ Click Print when you are satisfied with the layout.

Excel prints out the selected areas.

TIP

Delete It!
To clear the print area, click the Page Layout tab and then click Print Area. In the menu that appears, click Clear Print Area. Print areas stay in effect until you clear them. You can add to the print area by selecting a range and then clicking the Page Layout tab. Click Print Area, and then click Add to Print Area.

Print Multiple Worksheets from a Workbook

By default, Excel prints either the entire active worksheet or a selected print area within the worksheet. However, you can select several worksheet tabs and print them all at the same time. You may want to use this option if you have a workbook with data or charts on several separate sheets.

When you select multiple tabs, Excel groups the sheets. While the sheets are grouped, any data you type in any sheet, or any change you make to the structure of a sheet, are also typed into or changed in all the other sheets in the group.

To ungroup sheets, right-click any sheet. In the menu that appears, click Ungroup Sheets.

---

① Press and hold the Ctrl key.

② Click the individual tabs you want to print.

  You can click Chart tabs, Sheet tabs, and tabs you have renamed.

③ Release the Ctrl key.

  The selected tabs appear white.

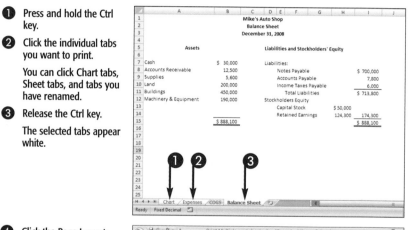

④ Click the Page Layout tab.

⑤ Click the Page Setup group launcher.

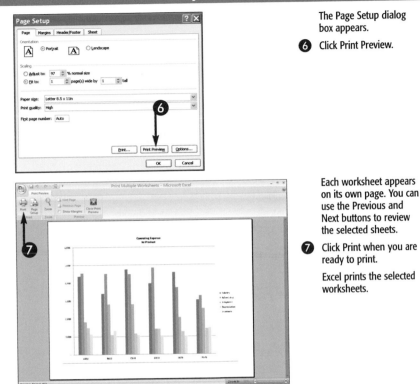

The Page Setup dialog box appears.

6 Click Print Preview.

Each worksheet appears on its own page. You can use the Previous and Next buttons to review the selected sheets.

7 Click Print when you are ready to print.

Excel prints the selected worksheets.

TIP

Did You Know?

You can print several workbooks at the same time. Simply click the Microsoft Office button and then click Open. In the Open dialog box, press and hold the Ctrl key and click the workbooks you want to print. Click the Tools drop-down menu in the lower-right corner, and then click Print.

Extending Excel

In Excel, you can do more than create and maintain workbooks and worksheets. Through data exchange, you can extend Excel in two ways. First, you can use data from other programs within Excel and thereby apply Excel's extensive worksheet capabilities to other programs' data. Second, you can use Excel data within other programs, thereby extending your ability to use, analyze, and present your Excel data.

This chapter focuses on the many techniques for integrating Excel with Word, PowerPoint, and Access, querying Websites, importing data, and querying Access databases from Excel.

With queries, you can bring non-Excel data, such as a Microsoft Access table, into Excel. As you create a query, you can sort and

filter the data. Later, you can analyze and chart the data as you would any other worksheet data. Queries are a powerful database tool for analyzing data sets.

With minor changes, you can extend the tasks in this chapter to exchange data with corporate databases based on Oracle, SQL Server, and other such products.

Less known to Excel users are the query features that enable you to query a Website within Excel. You can query a Website and import Web content into Excel, such as statistics presented in HTML tables that are in tabular format.

You can create hyperlinks from your worksheets to other worksheets and other programs. You can also use a hyperlink to open a related workbook or to open a related Word document.

Quick Tips

Paste Link into Word or PowerPoint 170

Embed a Worksheet...172

Hyperlink a Worksheet..174

Query a Website 176

Import a Text File 178

Import an Access Database...182

Query an Access Database 184

Reuse a Saved Query...188

Export a Worksheet to Access 190

By Paste linking Excel worksheets into Word or PowerPoint, you can add sophisticated calculations that you create in Excel to documents that you create in Word or PowerPoint. For example, in Word you can use Excel worksheets to present quarterly reports or other financial documents.

When you Paste link, if you alter Excel data in Word or PowerPoint, Office

automatically updates the Excel source document. The opposite is also true: When you alter Paste-linked data in Excel, Office automatically updates the linked Word or PowerPoint document. Paste linking enables you to keep your documents in sync because you do not have to worry about manually coordinating the changes in one document with changes in the other document.

① Select the worksheet data you want to Paste link.

② Click the Copy icon.

③ Switch to the Word document.

④ Click the Home tab.

⑤ Click Paste.

A menu appears.

⑥ Click Paste Special.

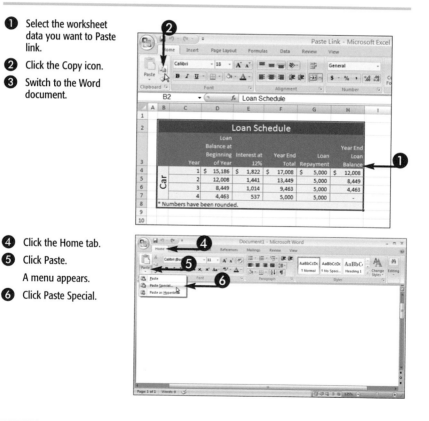

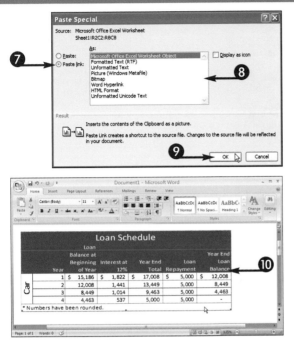

The Paste Special dialog box appears.

7 Click Paste link.

8 Click a Paste link option.

This example uses the Microsoft Office Excel Worksheet Object.

9 Click OK.

The worksheet appears in Word.

10 Double-click to edit the worksheet.

Your worksheet opens in Excel, and you can make any necessary edits.

When you have completed your edits, close Excel, and return to your Word document.

TIP

Did You Know?

This task Paste links an Excel worksheet into Word. You can follow the same steps to Paste link an Excel worksheet into PowerPoint; just switch to PowerPoint instead of Word in step 3.

When you create a PowerPoint presentation or a Word document, you can edit your worksheets without leaving PowerPoint or Word. This means you can demonstrate different business scenarios as you give your PowerPoint presentation, or do sophisticated mathematical calculations while in Word.

To use this feature, you must embed your worksheet into your PowerPoint or Word file. You can use an existing Excel file or generate a new file entirely within PowerPoint or Word.

When you embed an Excel document, the Excel worksheet becomes part of the PowerPoint or Word document and is accessible only through PowerPoint or Word. Embedding differs from Paste linking. When you make changes to an embedded Excel document, the changes only affect the PowerPoint or Word file.

① Open the PowerPoint presentation in which you want to include a worksheet.

Note: This example uses PowerPoint. You can follow similar steps to embed your document in Word.

② Click the Insert tab.

③ Click the Insert Object icon.

The Insert Object dialog box appears.

④ Click to select the Create new option to generate a new worksheet.

Alternatively, click the Create from file option to open an existing workbook.

⑤ Click Microsoft Office Excel Worksheet.

⑥ Click OK.

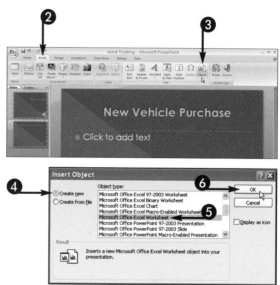

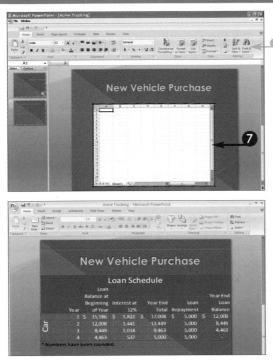

A blank worksheet appears.

● All of the Microsoft Excel commands are available to you.

⑦ Create your worksheet.

Click outside the worksheet when you have finished.

Excel adds the worksheet to your PowerPoint presentation.

Did You Know?

When you create a new Excel chart in PowerPoint, you see a fake data set and associated chart. Change the data and replace it with your own, either by typing in new data or by copying and pasting data from part of an existing Excel worksheet. You can use the new or copied data as the basis for a chart that you can modify as you would any chart. For more information on creating charts, see Chapter 6.

Hyperlink a Worksheet

You are probably familiar with the many benefits of links on Web pages. When you click a link, you jump to a new Web page with more links, creating an enormous and seamless web of information. Like most Office applications, Excel also lets you create links. These links can take users to a place in the same worksheet or workbook, to a document created by another Office application, or even to a Web page.

You can use links to jump directly to a chart or PivotTable based on the worksheet. You can also link a worksheet to a Word document that provides detailed information or identifies the assumptions used in the worksheet.

---

① Click the cell in which you want the hyperlink to appear.

② Click the Insert tab.

③ Click Hyperlink.

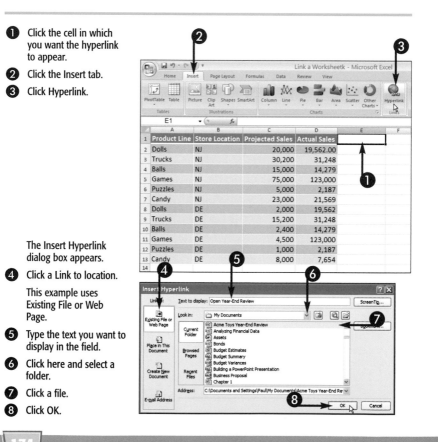

The Insert Hyperlink dialog box appears.

④ Click a Link to location.

This example uses Existing File or Web Page.

⑤ Type the text you want to display in the field.

⑥ Click here and select a folder.

⑦ Click a file.

⑧ Click OK.

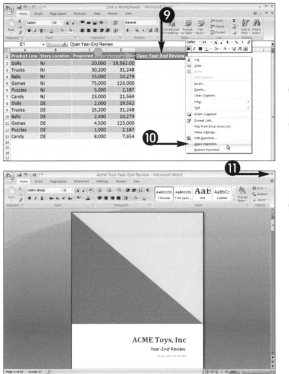

● The cell content appears as a hyperlink. You can pass your mouse over the link without clicking to see the name of the linked-to file.

❾ Right-click the link.

A menu appears.

❿ Click Open Hyperlink.

The linked-to document appears.

⓫ Close the document to return to your original document.

To remove the hyperlink, right-click the linked worksheet cell and then click Remove Hyperlink.

TIP

Did You Know?
You can create hyperlinks from workbook images such as shapes, pictures, clip art, and WordArt. Click the object, click the Insert tab, and then click Hyperlink. Use the Insert Hyperlink dialog box to select a destination in the same document, in another document, or on the Web.

You can import and use Web-based data in Excel by querying a Website. Importing data as a query enables you to filter the data, thus allowing you to view only records of interest. A query also lets you refresh data if it is subject to updates. With the data in Excel, you have complete access to data analysis and presentation tools, including functions, PivotTables, and charts.

You can find structured data in many forms on the Web, including online Excel worksheets. Even ordinary Web pages can be considered structured if they contain tabular content — that is, rows and columns of numbers or other data.

① Open a new Excel worksheet.

② Click the Data tab.

③ Click From Web.

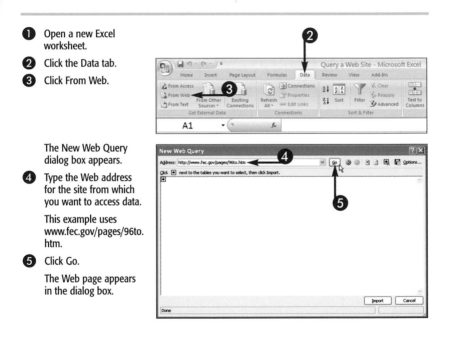

The New Web Query dialog box appears.

④ Type the Web address for the site from which you want to access data.

This example uses www.fec.gov/pages/96to.htm.

⑤ Click Go.

The Web page appears in the dialog box.

New Web Query

Address: http://www.fec.gov/pages/96to.htm

Click [+] next to the tables you want to select, then click Import.

⑥oter Registration and Turnout - 1996

☑ STATE	1996 VAP	1996 REG	% REG of VAP	TURNOUT*	% T/O of VAP
Alabama	3,220,000	2,470,766	76.73%	1,534,349	47.65%
Alaska	425,000	414,815	97.60%	241,620	56.85%
Arizona	3,145,000	2,244,672	71.37%	⑦1,404,405	44.66%

Import   Cancel

Done

⑥ Click the elements you do not want to appear in your query.

A check mark indicates you want to query an element. An arrow indicates you do not want to query it.

⑦ Click Import.

Import Data

Where do you want to put the data?
⦿ Existing worksheet:
=$A$1 ◀——⑧
○ New worksheet

Properties...   OK   Cancel

⑨

The Import Data dialog box appears.

⑧ Click to select a location for the imported page.

⑨ Click OK.

The selected Web elements appear within Excel, ready for analysis and charting.

Did You Know?
To find statistical data on the Web, you can do a Google search. You can download U.S. federal statistics in multiple formats from the official FedStats site at www.fedstats.gov/cgi-bin/A2Z.cgi. State and municipal data are also widely available. You can find central access to this material at the federal compendium, FirstGov, available at www.firstgov.gov.

Many software applications have an option you can use to export the application's data to a text file. You can then import text files from other applications into Excel by using the Text Import Wizard.

You can use Excel's sophisticated data analysis capabilities to analyze the data. In fact, once you have imported the data, you can use it in a PivotTable, create

charts with it, or manipulate it just as you would any other Excel data.

The Text Import Wizard can handle any delimited or fixed-width file. A delimited file uses a comma, semicolon, tab, space, or other character to mark the end of each column. A fixed-width file aligns each column and gives each column a defined width.

---

① Click the Data tab.

② Click From Text.

The Import Text File dialog box appears.

③ Click here and locate the folder in which you stored your file.

④ Click the file.

⑤ Click Import.

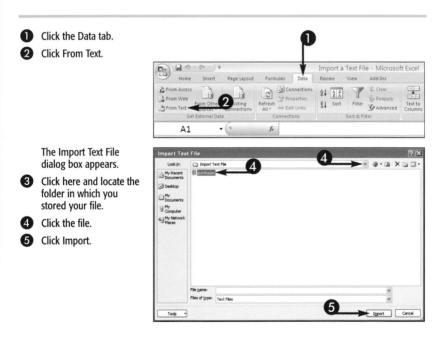

The Text Import Wizard appears.

⑥ Click to select the file type that best describes your data.

⑦ Click to select the row at which to begin importing.

⑧ Click Next.

⑨ Click to select the type of delimiter your data uses.

⑩ Click to select the text qualifier your data uses.

⑪ Click Next.

Did You Know?

On the first page of the Data Import Wizard, there is a field you can use to specify the row in your text file where you want to begin the import. If your data has titles or other information you do not want to import at the top of the file, you can skip those rows.

continued

If you are importing a fixed-width file, you tell Excel where each column begins by clicking the location in the Data Preview window. If you are importing a delimited file, you tell Excel the type of delimiters the file uses. Some delimited file formats surround text data with a text qualifier. The Text Import Wizard provides you with a field in which you can

specify whether your data has a text qualifier, and if so, what the qualifier is.

After you have defined the layout of your data, you define the data type that is contained in each column. You have three options: general, text, and date. If there is a column you do not want to import, click to select the Do not import column option.

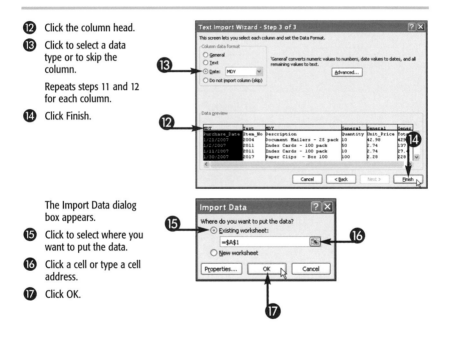

⑫ Click the column head.

⑬ Click to select a data type or to skip the column.

Repeats steps 11 and 12 for each column.

⑭ Click Finish.

The Import Data dialog box appears.

⑮ Click to select where you want to put the data.

⑯ Click a cell or type a cell address.

⑰ Click OK.

	A	B	C	D	E	F	G
1	Purchase_Date	Item_No	Description	Quantity	Unit_Price	Total_Price	
2	1/21/2007	2004	Document Mailers - 25 pack	10	42.98	429.8	
3	1/2/2007	2011	Index Cards - 100 pack	50	2.74	137	
4	1/11/2007	2011	Index Cards - 100 pack	10	2.74	27.4	
5	1/30/2007	2017	Paper Clips - Box 100	100	2.28	228	
6	1/26/2007	2035	Razor Point Pens - Box 12	12	12.49	149.88	
7	1/22/2007	2038	CD/DVD Envelopes - 25 pack	50	5.78	289	
8	1/10/2007	2040	Self Sealing Envelopes - 100 pack	25	20.78	519.5	
9	1/9/2007	2042	Hanging Data Binders - Each	50	4.39	219.5	
10	1/26/2007	2048	Desk Stapler - Each	24	15.75	378	
11							
12							

Excel imports your data.

	A	B	C	D	E	F	G
1	Purchase_Dat	Item_No	Description	Quantit	Unit_Price	Total_Price	
2	1/21/2007	2004	Document Mailers - 25 pack	10	42.98	429.8	
3	1/2/2007	2011	Index Cards - 100 pack	50	2.74	137	
4	1/11/2007	2011	Index Cards - 100 pack	10	2.74	27.4	
5	1/30/2007	2017	Paper Clips - Box 100	100	2.28	228	
6	1/26/2007	2035	Razor Point Pens - Box 12	12	12.49	149.88	
7	1/22/2007	2038	CD/DVD Envelopes - 25 pack	50	5.78	289	
8	1/10/2007	2040	Self Sealing Envelopes - 100 box	25	20.78	519.5	
9	1/9/2007	2042	Hanging Data Binders - Each	50	4.39	219.5	
10	1/26/2007	2048	Desk Stapler - Each	24	15.75	378	
11							
12							

You can format and analyze your data.

TIP

Did You Know?

Excel has an option you can use to break individual cells into columns. This feature works a lot like the Text Import Wizard. You select the field you want to divide, and then you click Text to Columns on the Data tab. The Convert Text to Columns Wizard opens. Use it to divide your cells into columns.

Many organizations use more than one application to manage structured data. Excel is excellent for managing, analyzing, and presenting numbers.

In Access, instead of using worksheets, you carefully organize your information into data tables, each of which stores information about one part of the entity of interest to you, such as customers, products, employees, and transactions. To help keep track of these tables in Access, you create unique identifiers, called keys. The keys link tables to each other.

Excel simplifies the use of Access data tables. When you import a data table, you can select tables or columns of interest from multiple tables, and display the results in a single worksheet.

① Open the workbook in which you want to view Access data.

② Click the Data tab.

③ From Access.

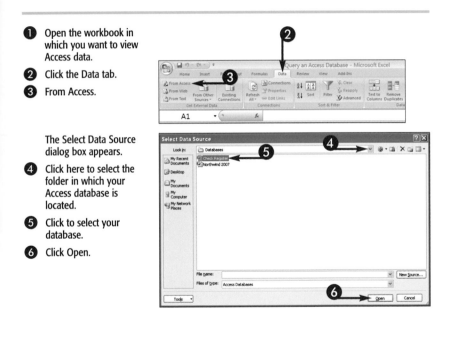

The Select Data Source dialog box appears.

④ Click here to select the folder in which your Access database is located.

⑤ Click to select your database.

⑥ Click Open.

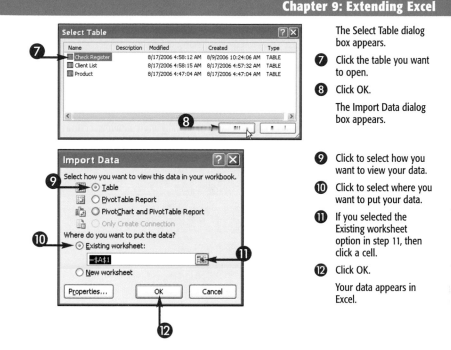

The Select Table dialog box appears.

⑦ Click the table you want to open.

⑧ Click OK.

The Import Data dialog box appears.

⑨ Click to select how you want to view your data.

⑩ Click to select where you want to put your data.

⑪ If you selected the Existing worksheet option in step 11, then click a cell.

⑫ Click OK.

Your data appears in Excel.

TIP

Did You Know?
This task uses the Northwind database, a large database that has been developed over many years and is distributed with Access on the Office CD. The database includes information about the products, customers, employees, and other attributes of a fictional gourmet food store. To follow along with this task or to experiment with importing and querying a database, you can install the Northwind database.

Query an Access Database

The Query Wizard is part of Microsoft Query, a separate application that comes with Microsoft Office. Microsoft Query makes it easy for you to generate queries in Structured Query Language (SQL), a standard language in the corporate world.

Using the Query Wizard, you can create multiple filters by using and and or. You use or when you want the wizard to

select data that meets either condition. For example, you can ask the wizard to select all dresses that are blue *or* have red buttons. Alternatively, you can ask the wizard to select all dresses that are blue *and* have red buttons. The and selection criteria are more restrictive. The wizard only returns items that meet both selection criteria: blue dresses with red buttons.

---

① Click the New Database Query icon.

Note: *You must install the New Database Query icon on the Quick Access toolbar. See Chapter 10 to learn how to install objects on the Quick Access toolbar.*

The Choose Data Source dialog box appears.

② Click the Databases tab.

③ Click MS Access Database*.

④ Click OK.

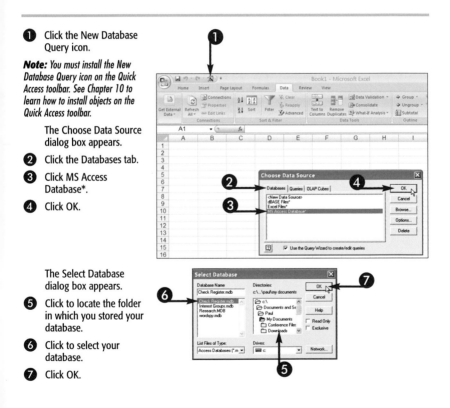

The Select Database dialog box appears.

⑤ Click to locate the folder in which you stored your database.

⑥ Click to select your database.

⑦ Click OK.

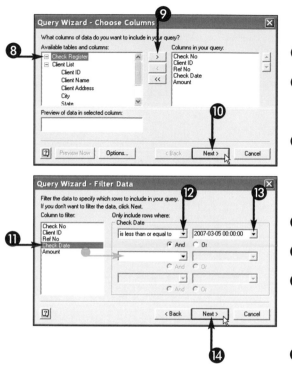

The Query Wizard –
Choose Columns dialog
box appears.

8 Click the table and fields
you want to import.

9 Click the Add button.

If you want to open
more than one table,
repeat steps 8 and 9.

10 Click Next.

The Query Wizard –
Filter Data dialog box
appears.

11 Click the column by
which you want to filter.

12 Click here and select a
comparison operator.

13 Click here and select the
criteria by which you
want to filter.

● You can apply additional
filters.

14 Click Next.

TIP

Important!
In this task, you click the New Database Query icon to access the
Choose Data Source dialog box. The task assumes that you have
installed the New Database Query icon on the Quick Access toolbar. See
Chapter 10 to learn how to add commands to the Quick Access toolbar.

You can create sorts within sorts using the Query Wizard. For example, you can alphabetize a list of states and counties as follows: first in alphabetical order by state, then in alphabetical order by county. After you import your data into Excel, you can use Excel's tools to further sort and filter.

On the final page of the wizard, you can click View data or edit query in Microsoft

Query and click Finish for a graphical view of the underlying data tables. After you create a query, you can save it.

You can add the Query Wizard to the Quick Access toolbar by adding the New Database Query icon. See Chapter 10 to learn how to add commands to the Quick Access toolbar.

⑮ Click here and select the column by which you want to sort your data.

⑯ Click to select either the Ascending or Descending order option.

● Optionally, you can add other sort criteria.

⑰ Click Next.

The Query Wizard – Finish dialog box appears.

⑱ Click to select the Return Data to Microsoft Office Excel option.

● Click View data or edit query in Microsoft Query and then Finish for a graphical view of the underlying data tables.

● Click here to save your query.

⑲ Click Finish.

The Import Data dialog box appears.

㉑ Click to select how you want to view your data.

㉑ Click to select where you want to place your data.

● If you selected the Existing worksheet option, then you can click and drag or type a range.

㉒ Click OK.

Your Access data appears in Excel.

	A	B	C	D	E	F
1	Check No	Client ID	Ref No	Check Date	Amount	
2	50247	CL-324	11150	3/1/2007 0:00	231.69	
3	50236	CL-300	11139	3/1/2007 0:00	605.71	
4	50234	CL-305	11137	3/1/2007 0:00	1015.15	
5	50248	CL-329	11151	3/1/2007 0:00	1461.02	
6	50242	CL-323	11145	3/1/2007 0:00	1817.57	
7	50241	CL-300	11144	3/1/2007 0:00	1852.42	
8	50245	CL-310	11148	3/1/2007 0:00	1996.15	
9	50246	CL-300	11149	3/1/2007 0:00	2941.65	
10	50249	CL-315	11152	3/1/2007 0:00	2979.46	
11	50239	CL-330	11142	3/1/2007 0:00	3143.82	
12	50243	CL-317	11146	3/1/2007 0:00	3284.35	
13	50235	CL-300	11138	3/1/2007 0:00	3379.4	
14	50244	CL-329	11147	3/1/2007 0:00	3606.71	
15	50240	CL-318	11143	3/1/2007 0:00	3928.45	
16	50238	CL-323	11141	3/1/2007 0:00	4691.22	
17	50250	CL-308	11153	3/1/2007 0:00	4770.37	
18	50237	CL-302	11140	3/1/2007 0:00	4810.37	
19	50258	CL-322	11161	3/2/2007 0:00	89.83	
20	50260	CL-310	11163	3/2/2007 0:00	293.47	
21	50262	CL-300	11165	3/2/2007 0:00	445.39	
22	50257	CL-306	11160	3/2/2007 0:00	837.58	
23	50255	CL-305	11158	3/2/2007 0:00	1165.32	
24	50252	CL-314	11155	3/2/2007 0:00	2168.92	
25	50261	CL-308	11164	3/2/2007 0:00	3419.17	
26	50256	CL-316	11159	3/2/2007 0:00	3529.75	
27	50254	CL-307	11157	3/2/2007 0:00	3745.93	

TIP

Did You Know?
On the final page of the Query Wizard, if you click View data or edit query in Microsoft Query and then click Finish, Excel provides a sophisticated interface you can use to edit your query. Click Help on the Microsoft Query menu to learn how to use this function.

Running a query has benefits beyond opening a database in Excel. For large databases, you can use filters to restrict which rows and columns you view. By saving the query, you can quickly return to the queried data, refresh the data, and perform all worksheet operations, such as applying functions, using PivotTables, and creating charts. Refreshing updates the

data so that you can see any changes made to the data in Access since the last refresh.

You can import queries into existing or new worksheets. After you import them, they look like any other worksheet. Saving changes in a workbook file leaves the original query definition untouched so that you can reuse it later.

① Open your Excel worksheet.

② Click the Data tab.

③ Click Existing Connections.

The Existing Connections dialog box appears.

④ Click the name of your saved query.

⑤ Click Open.

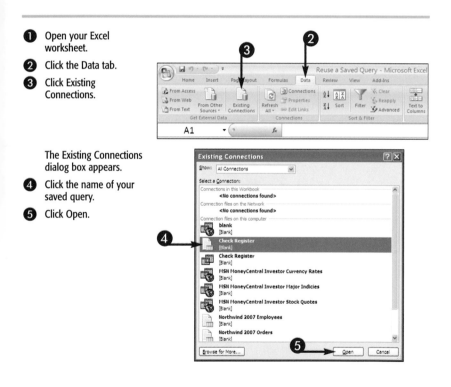

The Import Data dialog box appears.

6 Click to select how you want to view your data.

7 Click to select where you want to place your data.

● If you selected the Existing worksheet option, you can click and drag or type a range.

8 Click OK.

The results of your query appear in your worksheet.

9 Click the Data tab.

10 Click Refresh All.

Excel refreshes your data.

	A	B	C	D	E	F
1	Check No	Client ID	Ref No	Check Date	Amount	
2	50234	CL-305	11137	3/1/2007	1015.15	
3	50235	CL-300	11138	3/1/2007	3379.4	
4	50236	CL-300	11139	3/1/2007	605.71	
5	50237	CL-302	11140	3/1/2007	4810.37	
6	50238	CL-323	11141	3/1/2007	4691.22	
7	50239	CL-330	11142	3/1/2007	3143.82	
8	50240	CL-318	11143	3/1/2007	3928.45	
9	50241	CL-300	11144	3/1/2007	1852.42	
10	50242	CL-323	11145	3/1/2007	1817.57	
11	50243	CL-317	11146	3/1/2007	3284.35	
12	50244	CL-329	11147	3/1/2007	3606.71	
13	50245	CL-310	11148	3/1/2007	1996.15	

TIP

Did You Know?
You can edit a saved query. Click the Data tab, click Get External Data, click From Other Sources, and then click From Microsoft Query. The Choose Data Source dialog box appears. Click the Queries tab, click your query name, and then click Open. The query is now available for you to edit.

Tables enable you to take advantage of basic database features such as sorting and filtering within Excel. By bringing Excel lists into Microsoft Access, you can better manage growing lists by taking advantage of additional database features.

Before exporting a worksheet into Access, you need to format it as a list. Your columns may have headings; however, you should try to eliminate blank columns, rows, and cells. Exported Excel lists should also avoid repeating information. For example, instead of including a customer's name and address in every record of a transaction list, you should split the worksheet into two lists: one with customer information and the other with transaction information. In Access, the two lists become two tables linked by a key field.

① Open a new database in Access.

② Click the External Data tab.

③ Click Excel.

The Get External Data – Excel Spreadsheet dialog box appears.

④ Type the path to the file you want to import.

● Alternatively, click the Browse button and locate your file.

⑤ Click OK.

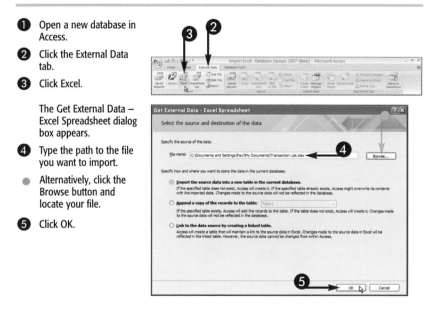

The Import Spreadsheet Wizard appears.

6 Click the worksheet you want to import.

7 Click Next.

The next page of the Import Spreadsheet Wizard appears.

8 Click if your data has column headings.

9 Click Next.

TIP

Did You Know?

When you export data, every row in each column should have the same data type. A column with more than one data type can cause errors during the export process. Access looks at a column's first eight rows to determine the column's data type.

Each record in an Access database must be unique. A primary key field is a field, such as a record number, that you use to ensure that a record is unique. You can have Access create primary key field values or you can create your own.

You use the Import Spreadsheet Wizard to import Excel data. The wizard enables

you to set several field options during the import process. For example, you can change field names and data types, or you can choose not to import a field.

You can index a field during the export process. An index speeds up the retrieval of information in Access.

The next page of the Import Spreadsheet Wizard appears.

⑩ Click to select a column heading.

⑪ Set the Field Options.

⑫ Click Next.

The next page of the Import Spreadsheet Wizard appears.

⑬ Click to set your primary key.

● If you choose to set your own primary key, click here and select a field.

⑭ Click Next.

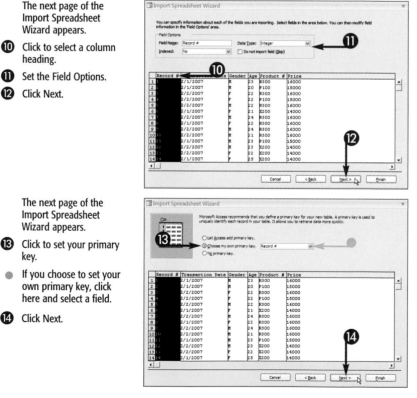

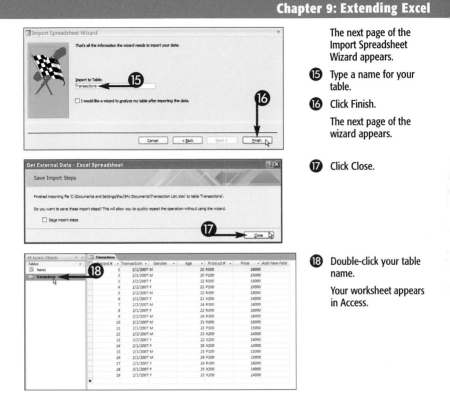

The next page of the Import Spreadsheet Wizard appears.

⑮ Type a name for your table.

⑯ Click Finish.

The next page of the wizard appears.

⑰ Click Close.

⑱ Double-click your table name.

Your worksheet appears in Access.

Did You Know?

You can append Excel data to an existing Access table. On the first page of the Get External Data – Excel Spreadsheet wizard, click Append a copy of the records to the table and then select the table to which you want to append the data.

Chapter 10

Customizing Excel

Excel has a large number of integrated features you can customize and adapt to suit your purposes. This chapter introduces a few important ways in which you can customize Excel.

One simple way is to install additional features, called *add-ins*. This chapter shows you how to install the add-ins included with Excel, and how to find add-ins available from third-party developers.

This chapter also shows you how to customize Excel by placing items on the Quick Access toolbar. Items on the Quick Access toolbar are independent of the tabs in the Ribbon, and you can access them with a single click. Many options that are not available in the Ribbon can be added to Excel through the Quick Access toolbar.

In addition, this chapter teaches you how to open multiple windows and create custom views. When using a large worksheet, you can open multiple windows to view different parts of the worksheet at the same time. If you filter data, hide columns or rows, or create special print settings, you can save your changes in a custom view and recall them when you need them. Another task shows you how to create a custom number format for use in a workbook.

The task on macros introduces an enormous topic, which enables you to extend and customize Excel more than any other task. After you learn how to create a macro, you learn how to assign a macro icon to the Quick Access toolbar.

Install Add-Ins 196

Customize the Quick Access Toolbar..............................198

Work with Multiple Windows...200

Save Time by Creating a Custom View 201

Create a Custom Number Format.....................................202

Automate a Worksheet with Macros................................204

Add an Icon to Run a Macro 206

An *add-in* is software that adds one or more features to Excel. Chapters 5 and 6 introduce a few of the statistical add-ins in the Analysis ToolPak. Bundled add-in software is software that is included with Excel but not automatically installed when you install Excel. You install the bundled add-ins by using the Add-Ins section of the Excel Options dialog box.

In addition, you can take advantage of third-party add-ins. This type of software adds functionality in support of advanced work in accounting, chemistry, risk analysis, project management, statistics, and other fields. Third-party add-ins usually have their own installation and usage procedures.

① Click the Microsoft Office button.

A menu appears.

② Click Excel Options.

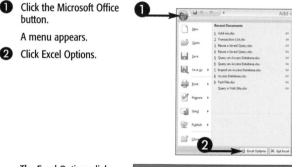

The Excel Options dialog box appears.

③ Click Add-Ins.

The View and manage Microsoft Office add-ins options appear.

④ Click an add-in.

⑤ Click Go.

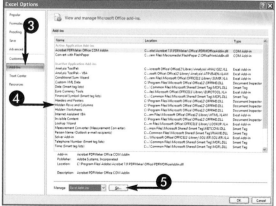

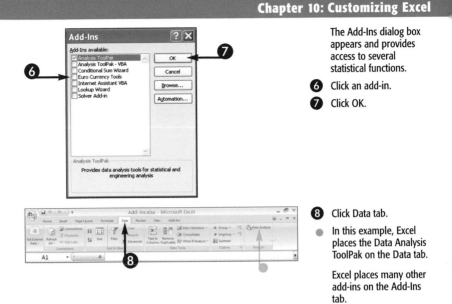

The Add-Ins dialog box appears and provides access to several statistical functions.

6 Click an add-in.

7 Click OK.

8 Click Data tab.

● In this example, Excel places the Data Analysis ToolPak on the Data tab.

Excel places many other add-ins on the Add-Ins tab.

Did You Know?

To learn about special-purpose Excel add-ins in your field, you can perform a Google search by going to www.google.com. Your search terms should include Excel, the field of knowledge — for example, chemistry, statistics, or accounting — the word add-ins, and other information you might have, such as the vendor name. Third-party vendors are responsible for supporting their own products.

You can add features you frequently use to the Microsoft Excel Quick Access toolbar. The Quick Access toolbar enables you to access commands with a single click.

Right clicking a Ribbon command provides you with a way to add commands in the Ribbon to the Quick Access toolbar easily. You can also add features that are not in the Ribbon to the

Quick Access toolbar by accessing the Excel Options dialog box Customize section and clicking the commands you want to add. You can customize the Quick Access toolbar for particular documents or for all documents. Several tasks in this book demonstrate features you must add to the Quick Access toolbar before you can use them.

① Click the Quick Access toolbar here.

② Click More Commands.

The Excel Options dialog box appears.

③ Click here and select a category.

④ Click the command you want to add to the Quick Access toolbar.

⑤ Click Add.

● The item moves to the list box on the right.

⑥ Click OK.

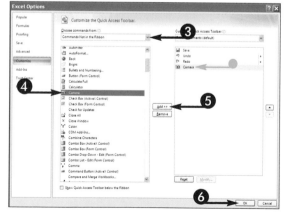

- Excel places the command on the Quick Access toolbar.

You can click the command to use it.

Note: This example uses the camera. See Chapter 7 to learn more about using the camera.

7 Right-click the command.

A menu appears.

8 Click Show Quick Access Toolbar Below the Ribbon.

- Excel places the Quick Access toolbar below the Ribbon.

Did You Know?
You should review all the options listed under Commands Not in the Ribbon. This is particularly true if you have used a previous version of Microsoft Excel. If a command from a previous version is not in the Ribbon, you may find it listed under Commands Not in the Ribbon.

Work with Multiple Windows

When a worksheet contains a lot of data, you cannot see all of it at the same time. Excel enables you to open additional copies of the worksheet, each in its own window, so you can view them simultaneously yet manipulate them independently.

By opening multiple copies of a worksheet, you can compare nonadjacent rows and columns. You can view the worksheets side by side, stacked, tiled, or cascaded. The zoom settings control how much of a worksheet appears on your screen.

① Click the View tab.

② Click New Window.

● Excel creates a new window.

③ Click Arrange All.

The Arrange Windows dialog box appears.

④ Click an Arrange option.

Click Horizontal to place the windows on top of each other.

Click Vertical to place the Windows side by side.

⑤ Click OK.

Excel displays both windows.

⑥ Click a window to activate it.

You can navigate each window independent of the others.

⑦ Drag to adjust the zoom.

Excel resizes the contents of the window.

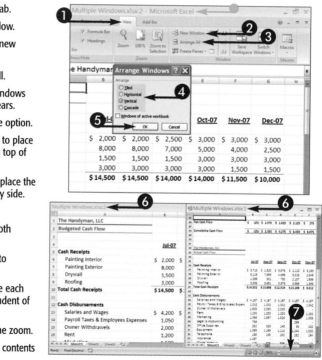

After you create a worksheet, you may want to filter your data, hide columns or rows, or create special print settings. For example, you may want to keep information on every quarter of a year in a single worksheet, but be able to present one quarter at a time.

You can filter your data, hide columns, set print settings, and save these settings by

creating a custom view. You can then recall the view whenever you need it.

To hide columns or rows, you must first select the columns or rows you want to hide and then use the Hide Rows or Hide Columns commands on the Home tab in the Cells Group under Format to hide them.

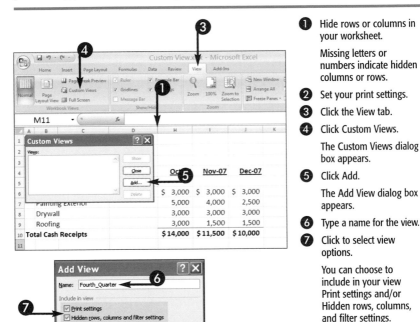

① Hide rows or columns in your worksheet.

Missing letters or numbers indicate hidden columns or rows.

② Set your print settings.

③ Click the View tab.

④ Click Custom Views.

The Custom Views dialog box appears.

⑤ Click Add.

The Add View dialog box appears.

⑥ Type a name for the view.

⑦ Click to select view options.

You can choose to include in your view Print settings and/or Hidden rows, columns, and filter settings.

⑧ Click OK.

Excel adds the view.

To use the view, open the workbook, click the View tab, click Custom Views, click the name of the saved view, and then click Show.

Create a Custom Number Format

Excel provides many formats for presenting numbers, dates, and times, as well as other numerical data. You can use these formats, or you can create custom formats.

Creating formats requires you use number codes, such as 0 or #, to stand for any digit. Use 0 if you want Excel to enter a 0 when you do not type any other number.

Use # when you only want the typed digit to appear. For example, to represent a social security number, you can use the code 000-00-0000.

When you type the numbers into the cell with the custom format, Excel adds the dashes automatically. To code text, simply place the text in quotes, for example, "SSN" 000-00-0000.

---

① Click the Home tab.

② Click the Number group launcher.

The Format Cells dialog box appears.

③ Click the Number tab.

④ Click a category with formats similar to the one you want to create.

⑤ Click a format type similar to the one you want to create.

⑥ Click Custom.

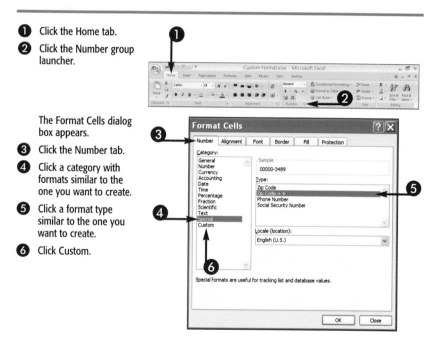

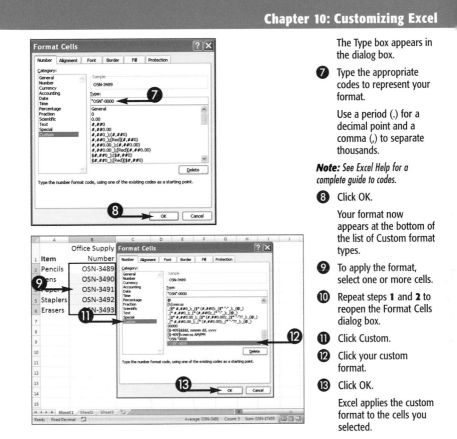

The Type box appears in the dialog box.

⑦ Type the appropriate codes to represent your format.

Use a period (.) for a decimal point and a comma (,) to separate thousands.

Note: *See Excel Help for a complete guide to codes.*

⑧ Click OK.

Your format now appears at the bottom of the list of Custom format types.

⑨ To apply the format, select one or more cells.

⑩ Repeat steps **1** and **2** to reopen the Format Cells dialog box.

⑪ Click Custom.

⑫ Click your custom format.

⑬ Click OK.

Excel applies the custom format to the cells you selected.

TIP

Caution!
Excel correctly applies custom number formats as long as you type the correct number of digits. For example, for the format ##-##, if you type too many digits, Excel correctly formats numbers starting from the right, but incorrectly formats the excess digits on the left.

Automate a Worksheet with Macros

A macro enables you to automate common tasks. You create a macro by recording each step of the task and then assigning all the steps to a keyboard shortcut. Pressing the assigned keyboard shortcut replays the steps.

To record a macro, you must turn on the Macro recorder. Excel records every keystroke, toolbar command, or menu command you execute. When you finish the task, turn off the Macro recorder.

You can create an icon, place it on the Quick Access toolbar, and then click the icon to run the macro. To find out how, see the next section, "Create an Icon to Run a Macro." When you save a workbook that contains a macro, you must save it as an Excel Macro-Enabled Workbook.

---

① Click to select a cell.

② Click the Record Macro button.

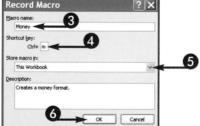

The Record Macro dialog box appears.

③ Type a name for the macro.

④ Type a letter to assign a keyboard shortcut.

You can press and hold Shift and a letter to assign a capitalized shortcut.

⑤ Click here and select the scope of your macro.

⑥ Click OK.

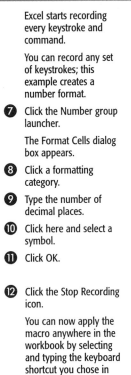

Excel starts recording every keystroke and command.

You can record any set of keystrokes; this example creates a number format.

⑦ Click the Number group launcher.

The Format Cells dialog box appears.

⑧ Click a formatting category.

⑨ Type the number of decimal places.

⑩ Click here and select a symbol.

⑪ Click OK.

⑫ Click the Stop Recording icon.

You can now apply the macro anywhere in the workbook by selecting and typing the keyboard shortcut you chose in step 4.

TIP

Did You Know?

By default, the Record Macro button appears on the status bar. You decide what options display on the status bar by right-clicking the bar. A menu appears. Select the options you want. When working with macros, make sure you select Macro Recording.

Create an Icon to Run a Macro

You can create an icon to run your macro. For a common task such as applying a format, a macro icon can speed up your work and help you avoid repeatedly opening a dialog box and making the same selections.

To assign a macro to an icon, you must first create the macro, as explained in the previous section, "Automate a Worksheet with Macros." You can then select an icon to represent the macro and move the icon to the Quick Access toolbar. Once the icon is on the Quick Access toolbar, you simply click the icon to run the macro.

As an alternative to running your macro with an icon, you can press Alt+F8 to open the Macro dialog box.

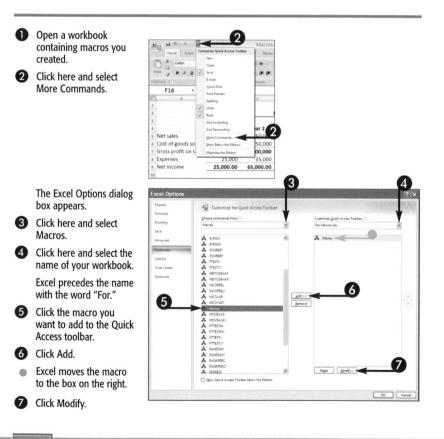

① Open a workbook containing macros you created.

② Click here and select More Commands.

The Excel Options dialog box appears.

③ Click here and select Macros.

④ Click here and select the name of your workbook.

Excel precedes the name with the word "For."

⑤ Click the macro you want to add to the Quick Access toolbar.

⑥ Click Add.

● Excel moves the macro to the box on the right.

⑦ Click Modify.

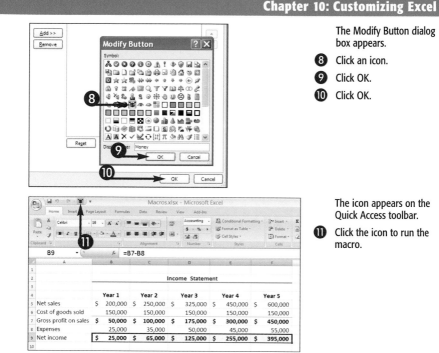

The Modify Button dialog box appears.

8 Click an icon.

9 Click OK.

10 Click OK.

The icon appears on the Quick Access toolbar.

11 Click the icon to run the macro.

Did You Know?

You can assign a macro to an image. Start by placing the image on your worksheet. Right-click the image. A menu appears. Right-click again. Another menu appears. Click Assign Macro. The Assign Macro dialog box appears. Click the macro you want to assign to the image and then click OK. Now you can click the image to run the macro.

Index

Symbols and Numbers

$ (dollar sign). *See* symbols.
- (hyphens). *See* symbols.
- (minus sign), on buttons, 14, 110
+ (plus sign), on buttons, 14, 110
" (quotation marks). *See* symbols.
{ } (curly braces), 35
error, 49
3-D charts, 126, 128–129
3-D rotations, 146–147

A

accepting reviewer changes, 69
Access data, 182–189
add-ins, 196–197
Add-Ins dialog box, 197
Advanced Filter dialog box, 76–77, 84–85
Allow Users to Edit Ranges dialog box, 159
Analysis ToolPak, 196–197
analyzing data. *See* PivotTables; *specific analyses.*
angles, pictures, 148–149
arithmetic operations, with Paste Special dialog box, 58–59
Arrange Windows dialog box, 200
arranging windows, 200
array functions, 35
arrays, 35, 41
arrows, 144–145
Assign Macro dialog box, 207
AutoFill feature, 10–11
average, calculating, 91, 115
AVERAGE function, 115

B

background graphics, 152–153
backward compatibility, 162–163
banded rows/columns, 96–97
banners, 144–145
bar charts, 130–131
bevels, 146–147
bins, 138–139
borders, pictures, 148–149
bottom N values, 32–33
brightness, pictures, 148–149
Browse dialog box, 71

C

calculated PivotTable fields, 108–109
calculations. *See specific calculations.*
calculator, 38–39
callouts, 144–145
Camera icon, on Quick Access toolbar, 155
cells
    breaking into columns, 181
    converting from tables, 95
    formatting, 106–107, 158–159
    naming, 4–5
    speaking contents of, 18–19
Chart Tools, 124–125
charts. *See also* PivotCharts.
    adding details, 126–129
    add/remove data, 134–135
    bins, 138–139
    creating, 124–125
    error bars, 136–137
    filtered data, 88–89
    histograms, 138–139
    legends, 135
    margin of error, 136–137
    trendlines, 132–133
    type, changing, 130–131
Choose Columns dialog box, 185
Choose Data Source dialog box, 184–185
clearing PivotTables, 113
Clipboard, 54–55
collapsing PivotTable data, 110
Color Scales, 66–67
colorizing photographs, 149
column charts, 130–131
column fields, PivotTables, 102–103
columns
    PivotTable, 102–103, 110
    table, 14–15, 52–53, 96–97
combination charts, 131
Commands Not in the Ribbon, 199
comments, 16–17
comparing nonadjacent rows/columns, 200
Compatibility Pack, 163
complex filters, 82–85
conditional
    formatting, 64–67
    formulas, 34–35
    sums, 36–37

Confirm Password dialog box, 159
Consolidate feature, 70–71
constants, 24–25, 27. See also formulas.
continuous data, 79
contrast, pictures, 148–149
Copy Picture dialog box, 154–155
Copy as Picture feature, 154–155
copying
    data to Clipboard, 54–55
    formats, 58–59
    formulas, 58–59
    image properties, 143
    keyboard shortcut, 57
    styles across workbooks, 62–63
    values, 58–59
CORREL (correlation) function, 116–117
correlations, identifying, 116–117
COUNTIF function, 37
counting, 37, 90–91
Create from Selection option, 4–5
Create PivotTable dialog box, 101
Create Table dialog box, 94–95
curly braces ({ }), 35
currency symbols, 12–13
custom number formats, 202–203
custom views, 201
customizing Excel, 196–207
cutting, keyboard shortcut, 57

D

data, PivotTables, 102–103, 104–105
Data Analysis dialog box, 114, 138–139
Data Bars, 65–67
data entry
    AutoFill feature, 10–11
    extending a series, 10–11
    with forms, 74–75
    PivotTables, 102–103
    rules, 8–9
    validating. See data validation.
Data Field Settings dialog box, 106–107
Data Import Wizard, 179
data validation, 6–9, 18–19
Data Validation dialog box, 6–7, 8–9
database queries, Access data, 184–187
dates. See also time.
    calculating days between, 44–45
    converting text values to, 51
    entering a series of, 10–11
    entering current, 45
    sorting chronologically, 80–81
DATEVALUE function, 49
DAVERAGE (database average) function, 91
DCOUNT (database count numeric) function, 90–91

DCOUNTA (database count non-numeric) function, 91
deleting
    constants, 25
    duplicate records, 76–77
    outlines, 15
    PivotChart filters, 113
delimited files, importing, 180–181
Descriptive Statistics dialog box, 115
discrete data, 79
displaying, constants, 25
#DIV/0 error, 49
dollar sign ($). See symbols.
drill-down button, 110
DSUM (database sum) function, 91
duplicate records, 76–77

E

Edit Series dialog box, 135
editing
    constants, 25
    database queries, 187
    forms, 75
    saved database queries, 189
entering data. See data entry.
error bars, 136–137
Evaluate Formula dialog box, 48–49
Excel Bible, 43
Excel Options dialog box, 196–197
Existing Connection dialog box, 188–189
expanding PivotTable data, 110
exporting, worksheets to Access, 190–193
extending a series of data, 10–11

F

FedStats site, 177
field headers, 109
Field List display, modifying, 103
Fill Formatting Only option, 11
Fill Without Formatting option, 11
Filter Data dialog box, 185
filtered records, 83, 88–89, 90–91
filtering, 76–70, 82–85. See also hiding.
filters, 102–103, 113
financial calculations
    Goal Seek feature, 29, 120–121
    internal rate of return, 30–31
    What-If analysis, 118–119
financial calculations, loans
    goal seeking, 120–121
    internal rate of return, 30–31
    terms, 28–29
    what-if analysis, 118–119
fixed-width files, importing, 180–181
floors, charts, 128–129

Index

flowcharts, 144–145
fonts, 146–147
foreign letters, 12–13
Format Cells dialog box, 106–107, 158–159
Format Chart Area dialog box, 127
Format Error Bars dialog box, 137
Format Painter, 142–143
Format Trendline dialog box, 132–133
Format Walls dialog box, 128–129
formats, copying, 58–59
formatting. *See also* styles.
    Color Scales, 66–67
    conditional, 64–67
    Data Bars, 65–67
    filled cells, 11
    highlighting certain conditions, 64–67
    icon sets, 66–67
    selective display, 66–67
    with symbols, 12–13
    worksheets, 142–143
forms, 74–75
formula bar, hiding, 153
formulas. *See also* constants; functions.
    #### error, 49
    conditional, 34–35
    conditional sums, 36–37
    constant names, 26–27
    copying, 58–59
    counting values, 37
    #DIV/0 error, 49
    error checking, 48–49
    #N/A error, 49
    nesting, 48–49
    range names, 4–5, 26–27
    symbols in, 12
    text values in, 50–51
    #VALUE error, 49
FREQUENCY function, 139. *See also* histograms.
Full Screen mode, 152–153
Function Arguments dialog box, 22–23, 29, 37, 117
Function Wizard, 22–23
functions. *See also* formulas; *specific functions.*
    array, 35
    searching for, 23
    statistical, 114–115
    using, 22–23

G

Get External Data dialog box, 190–193
glows, 146–147
Go To Special dialog box, 7
Goal Seek feature, 29, 120–121
grand totals, PivotTables, 106–107
graphics. *See* worksheets, graphics.
grayscale, photographs, 149
gridlines, hiding, 153
grouping
    graphics, 151
    hiding table rows/columns, 14–15
    rows/columns, PivotTables, 110
    worksheets, 166–167
GROWTH function, 133

H

headings, hiding, 153
Hidden and Empty Cell Settings dialog box, 88–89
hiding data. *See also* filtering.
    charts, 88–89
    rows/columns, PivotTables, 110
    rows/columns, worksheets, 14–15
    with subtotals, 86–87
highest values, 33
Highlight Changes dialog box, 68–69
highlighting, 64–67, 96–97
Histogram dialog box, 139
histograms, 138–139. *See also* FREQUENCY function.
hyperlinking worksheets to, Word, 174–175
hyphens (-). *See* symbols.

I

icon sets, 66–67
IF function, 34–35
images. *See* photographs; pictures; worksheets,
graphics.
Import Data dialog box, 187
Import Spreadsheet Wizard, 191
Import Text File dialog box, 178–181
importing worksheet data. *See* worksheets, importing.
Insert Calculated Field dialog box, 108–109
Insert Chart dialog box, 112–113
Insert Function dialog box, 22–23, 28–29

Insert Hyperlink dialog box, 174–175
Insert Picture dialog box, 148–149
internal rate of return, 30–31
IRR (Internal Rate of Return) function, 30–31

L

labels, 102–103, 111, 128–129
LARGE function, 32–33
largest values, calculating, 32–33
layout, PivotTables, 102–103, 105
legends, charts, 135
line charts, 130–131
lines (graphic), 144–145
loan calculations, 28–31, 118–121
locking, worksheets, 158–159
logos, 146–147
lookup, 92–93
lowest values, 33

M

macros, 204–207
margin of error, charts, 136–137
MAX (maximum) function, 33
mean, calculating, 91, 115
median, calculating, 115
MEDIAN function, 115
Merge Styles dialog box, 63
merging styles, 62–63
Microsoft Query, 184–185
MIN (minimum) function, 33
minus sign (-), on buttons, 14, 110
MOD (modulus) function, 43
mode, calculating, 115
MODE function, 115
moving, pictures, 148–149
multiplication, PRODUCT function, 40–41
multiplying, values of arrays, 41

N

#N/A error, 49
Name Manager, 4–5
naming
    cells, 4–5
    constants, 25–27
    ranges, 4–5, 25–27
    styles, 63
nesting formulas, 48–49
NETWORKDAY function, 44–45
New dialog box, 160–161
New Formatting Rule dialog box, 66–67
New Name dialog box, 4–5, 24–25

New Web Query dialog box, 176–177
New Workbook dialog box, 160–161
Northwind database, 183
number formats, custom, 202–203

O

older Excel versions, 162–163
outlines, 14–15
outlining feature, 14–15
overlapping graphics, 150–151

P

Page Setup dialog box, 164–165
passwords, worksheets, 158–159
Paste linking into Word or PowerPoint, 170–171
Paste Special dialog box, 52–53, 56–59, 171
Paste Special Validation option, 6–7
pasting, keyboard shortcut, 57
patterns in data. See PivotTables.
payment (PMT) function, 28–29, 118–119
perspective, charts, 126–127
photographs, 148–149. See also shapes; worksheets, graphics.
pictures, 148–149, 154–155. See also shapes; worksheets, graphics.
pie charts, 130–131
PivotCharts, 112–113, 137. See also charts; PivotTables.
PivotTables. See also PivotCharts.
    calculated fields, 108–109
    clearing, 113
    creating, 100–103
    data, modifying, 104–105
    grand totals, 106–107
    grouping rows/columns, 110
    hiding rows/columns, 110
    layout, modifying, 105
    Refresh button, 104
    refreshing, 104
    sorting, 111
    subtotals, 106–107
    summary statistics, 106–107
    ungrouping rows/columns, 110
plus sign (+), on buttons, 14, 110
PMT (payment) function, 28–29, 118–119
PowerPoint
    embedding worksheets, 172–173
    Paste linking into, 170–171
printing, 164–167
PRODUCT function, 40–41
products, calculating, 40–41
protecting, worksheets, 158–159

Index

Q

Query Wizard, 184–187
querying, 176–177, 184–187
Quick Access toolbar, customizing, 198–199
quotation marks ("). *See* symbols.

R

ranges, named. *See* naming, ranges.
read back data, 18–19
Record Macro dialog box, 204–205
rectangles, 144–145
red triangle comment indicator, 17
reflections, 146–147, 148–149
Refresh button, 104
refreshing PowerPoint data, 104
rejecting reviewer changes, 69
Remove Duplicates dialog box, 76–77
removing. *See* deleting.
renaming, constants, 25
report fields, PivotTables, 102–103
report filters, PivotTables, 102–103
reports. *See* printing.
restricting data entry, 6–9
reusing database queries, 188–189
Ribbon commands, 198–199
rotation, 126–127, 146–149
ROUND function, 22–23
rounding values, 22–23
row fields, PivotTables, 102–103
rows
    PivotTable, 102–103, 110
    table, 14–15, 52–53, 96–97
R-squared statistic, 132–133

S

saving
    database queries, 188–189
    system settings, 201
    workbooks as other formats, 162–163
    workbooks as templates, 160–161
Scenario Manager, 118–119
scientific calculations, 39
scope of constants, 24–25
searching, 75, 92–93
Select Data Source dialog box, 134–135, 182–183
Select Database dialog box, 184–185

Select Table dialog box, 183
Selection and Visibility pane, 150–151
selective display, 66–67
sepia tones, photographs, 149
shadows, 146–147, 148–149
shapes, in worksheets, 144–145. *See also* photographs; pictures.
Sheet Background dialog box, 152–153
SMALL function, 33
smallest values, calculating, 32–33
Sort By Value dialog box, 111
Sort dialog box, 78–79
sort levels, deleting and copying, 81
sorting, 78–81, 83, 86–87, 111
sorts, within sorts, 186–187
Speak Cells... icons, 18–19
special characters, 12–13
spoken data, 18–19
SQL (Structured Query Language), 184–185
SQRT (square root) function, 40–41
square roots, calculating, 40–41
stacking graphics, 150–151
standard deviation, calculating, 115
stars, 144–145
statistical functions, 114–115
statistics, online sources of, 177
STDEV (standard deviation) function, 115
Style dialog box, 60–61
styles. *See also* formatting.
    applying, 61
    charts, 124–125
    copying across workbooks, 62–63
    creating, 60
    merging, 62–63
    naming, 63
    pictures, 148–149
    tables, 96–97
subtotaling, 86–87, 106–107
SUMIF function, 36–37
summary statistics, 106–107
summing values, conditionally, 36–37
symbols, 12–13
synchronizing source and destination, 59

T

Table Tools, 94–95
tables, 94–97. *See also* PivotTables.

templates, 160–161
text boxes, 146–147
text files, importing, 178–181
text graphics, 147
Text Import Wizard, 178–181
text in
    formulas, 50–51
    pictures, 146–147
    shapes, 144–145
    worksheets, 146–147
3-D charts, 126, 128–129
3-D rotations, 146–147
time calculations, 42–43, 51. *See also* dates.
TIMEVALUE function, 49
top N values, 32–33
tracking reviewer changes, 68–69
TRANSPOSE function, 53
TREND function, 133
trendlines, 132–133

U

ungrouping
    rows and columns, 15
    rows/columns, PivotTables, 110
    worksheets, 166–167

V

validation lists, 6–7
#VALUE error, 49
values, copying, 58–59
Values box, 102–103
variables, correlations, 116–117
VLOOKUP (vertical lookup) function, 92–93

W

walls, charts, 128–129
Web-based data, importing, 176–177
What-If analysis, 118–119
Word
    embedding worksheets, 172–173
    hyperlinking worksheets, 174–175
    Paste linking into, 170–171
WordArt, 147
workbooks, 160–163

worksheets
    3-D rotations, 146–147
    Access data, importing, 182–183
    Access data, querying, 184–187
    banners, 144–145
    cells, breaking into columns, 181
    clearing the print area, 165
    consolidating, 70–71
    embedding in Word or PowerPoint, 172–173
    exporting to Access, 190–193
    flowcharts, 144–145
    fonts, 146–147
    formatting, 142–143
    formula bar, hiding, 153
    Full Screen mode, 152–153
    glows, 146–147
    graphics, 143–153. *See also* photographs;
        pictures.
    gridlines, hiding, 153
    grouping, 166–167
    headings, hiding, 153
    hyperlinking to Word, 174–175
    importing, 176–183
    locking, 158–159
    passwords, 158–159
    Paste linking into Word or PowerPoint, 170–171
    as pictures, 154–155
    printing multiple, 166–167
    printing noncontiguous areas, 164–165
    protecting, 158–159
    querying databases, 182–189
    querying Websites, 176–177
    sorts within sorts, 186–187
    text boxes, 146–147
    text graphics, 147
    text in pictures, 146–147
    text in shapes, 144–145
    transforms, 146–147
    ungrouping, 166–167
    WordArt, 147

X

.xls format, 162–163
.xlsx file extension, 160–161
.xltx file extension, 160–161